First World War
and Army of Occupation
War Diary
France, Belgium and Germany

31 DIVISION
Divisional Troops
211 Field Company Royal Engineers
28 February 1916 - 30 April 1919

WO95/2352/2

The Naval & Military Press Ltd
www.nmarchive.com
Published in association with The National Archives

Published by

The Naval & Military Press Ltd

Unit 10 Ridgewood Industrial Park,

Uckfield, East Sussex,

TN22 5QE England

Tel: +44 (0) 1825 749494

www.naval-military-press.com

www.nmarchive.com

This diary has been reprinted in facsimile from the original. Any imperfections are inevitably reproduced and the quality may fall short of modern type and cartographic standards.

© Crown Copyright
Images reproduced by permission of The National Archives, London, England, 2015.

Contents

Document type	Place/Title	Date From	Date To
Heading	WO95/2352/2		
Heading	31st Division Divl Engineers 211th Field Coy R.E. Mar 1916-Apr 1919		
Heading	War Diary Of 211th Field Company R.E. From 1.3.16 To 31.3.16 Apl 19		
War Diary	Kantara (Egypt)	28/02/1916	28/02/1916
War Diary	Kantara	01/03/1916	01/03/1916
War Diary	Marseille	06/03/1916	07/03/1916
War Diary	Pont Remy	09/03/1916	09/03/1916
War Diary	Hocquincourt	10/03/1916	24/03/1916
War Diary	Longpre	25/03/1916	25/03/1916
War Diary	Flesselles	26/03/1916	26/03/1916
War Diary	Beauval	27/03/1916	27/03/1916
War Diary	Mailly Maillet	28/03/1916	28/03/1916
War Diary	Englebelmer	29/03/1916	04/04/1916
War Diary	Bertrancourt	05/04/1916	31/05/1916
Miscellaneous	D.A.G. 3rd Echelon	12/07/1916	12/07/1916
War Diary	Bertrancourt	01/06/1916	11/06/1916
War Diary	Courcelles	12/06/1916	30/06/1916
Heading	Secret		
Heading	War Diary of 211th Fld. Coy. R.E. July 1st To July 31st. 1916 Volume VII		
War Diary	Courcelles	01/07/1916	05/07/1916
War Diary	Bus	06/07/1916	06/07/1916
War Diary	Beauval	07/07/1916	07/07/1916
War Diary	Candas	08/07/1916	08/07/1916
War Diary	Conteville	09/07/1916	09/07/1916
War Diary	Busnes	10/07/1916	15/07/1916
War Diary	L'Epinette	16/07/1916	17/07/1916
War Diary	Bout Deville	18/07/1916	24/07/1916
War Diary	Lacouture	25/07/1916	31/07/1916
Heading	War Diary Of 211th Field Company R.E. From 1.8.16 To 31.8.16 (Volume VIII)		
War Diary	Lacouture	01/08/1916	31/08/1916
Heading	War Diary 211th Field Coy. R.E. 31st Division September 1916 Vol 7		
War Diary	Lacouture	01/09/1916	30/09/1916
Heading	War Diary Of 211th Field Company R.E. From 1.10.16 To 31.10.16 (Volume 10)		
War Diary	Lacouture	01/10/1916	05/10/1916
War Diary	Calonne Sur La Lys	06/10/1916	09/10/1916
War Diary	Vauchelles	10/10/1916	17/10/1916
War Diary	Coigneux	18/10/1916	31/10/1916
Heading	War Diary 211th July Coy R.E. 31st Division Volume XI November 1916		
War Diary	Coigneux	01/11/1916	30/11/1916
Heading	War Diary Of 211th Field Company R.E. From Dec 1.16 To Dec 31.16 (Volume XII)		
War Diary	Coigneux	01/12/1916	31/12/1916

Type	Location/Title	Start	End
Heading	War Diary Of 211th Field Company R.E. From 1.1.17 To 31.1.17 (Volume 13)		
War Diary	Coigneux	01/01/1917	09/01/1917
War Diary	Bernaville	10/01/1917	31/01/1917
Heading	War Diary Of 211th Field Company R.E. From 1.2.17 To 28.2.17 (Volume XIV)		
War Diary	Bernaville	01/02/1917	05/02/1917
War Diary	Sailly Dell	06/02/1917	21/02/1917
War Diary	Bayencourt	22/02/1917	28/02/1917
Heading	War Diary Of 211th Field Company R.E. From March 1st 1917 To March 31st 1917 Volume 15		
War Diary	Bayencourt	01/03/1917	11/03/1917
War Diary	Courcelles	12/03/1917	18/03/1917
War Diary	Terramesnil	19/03/1917	19/03/1917
War Diary	Bretel	20/03/1917	20/03/1917
War Diary	Occoches	21/03/1917	21/03/1917
War Diary	Sibiville	22/03/1917	22/03/1917
War Diary	Grossart	23/03/1917	24/03/1917
War Diary	Fontaine-lez-Hermans	25/03/1917	25/03/1917
War Diary	St Venant	26/03/1917	31/03/1917
Heading	War Diary Of The 211th Field Coy. R.E. From April 1st 1917 To April. 30th 1917 Volume XVI		
War Diary	St Venant	01/04/1917	08/04/1917
War Diary	Gonnehem	09/04/1917	11/04/1917
War Diary	Maisnil-Lez-Ruitz	12/04/1917	14/04/1917
War Diary	Guestreville	15/04/1917	17/04/1917
War Diary	Ecoivres	18/04/1917	21/04/1917
War Diary	St Nicholas	22/04/1917	30/04/1917
Heading	War Diary Of 211th Field Company R.E. From May 1st 1917 To May 31st 1917 Volume XVII		
War Diary		01/05/1917	30/05/1917
Heading	War Diary Of 211th Field Company R.E. From June 1st 1917 To June 30th 1917 (Volume XVIII)		
War Diary	4 Vents M Arras	01/06/1917	30/06/1917
Heading	War Diary Of The 211th Field Company R.E. From 1st July 1917 To 31st July 1917 (Volume XIX) Original		
War Diary	St Nicholas	01/07/1917	04/07/1917
War Diary	ACQ	05/07/1917	13/07/1917
War Diary	Aux Rietz	14/07/1917	31/07/1917
Heading	War Diary Original Of 211th Field Company R.E. From 1st August 1917 To 31st August 1917 Volume XX		
War Diary	Aux Rietz	01/08/1917	31/08/1917
Heading	War Diary Of The 211th Field Coy R.E. From 1st Sept 1917 To 30th Sept 1917 (Volume XXI)		
War Diary	Aux Rietz	01/09/1917	08/09/1917
War Diary	Ecurie	09/09/1917	29/09/1917
Heading	War Diary Of The 211th Field Coy R.E. From 1st Oct 1917 To 31st Oct 1917 Volume XXII		
War Diary	Ecurie A27 a.7.6	01/10/1917	31/10/1917
Heading	War Diary Of The 211th Field Coy. R.E. From 1.11.17 To 30.11.17 Volume XXII		
War Diary	Ecurie	01/11/1917	30/11/1917
Heading	War Diary 211th Field Company R.E. 31st Division December 1917. Vol 22		
War Diary	Ecurie	01/12/1917	07/12/1917
War Diary	Mardeuil	08/12/1917	21/12/1917

War Diary	Ecurie	21/12/1917	31/12/1917
Heading	War Diary Of The 211th Field Company R.E. From 1st Jany 1918 To 31st Jan 1918 Volume XXV (Original)		
War Diary	Ecurie	01/01/1918	31/01/1918
Heading	War Diary Of 211th Field Company R.E. From 1st Feb 1918 To 28th Feb 1918 Volume XXVI (Original)		
War Diary	Ecurie	01/02/1918	28/02/1918
Heading	31st Divisional Engineers War Diary 211th Field Company R.E. March 1918		
Heading	War Diary Of 211th Field Company R.E. From 1/3/18 to 31/3/18 Volume XVII		
War Diary	Ecurie	01/03/1918	01/03/1918
War Diary	Maroeuil	02/03/1918	04/03/1918
War Diary	Brunehaut Farm	05/03/1918	11/03/1918
War Diary	Maroeuil	12/03/1918	22/03/1918
War Diary	Blaireville	23/03/1918	23/03/1918
War Diary	Courcelles-Le Comte	24/03/1918	25/03/1918
War Diary	Moncy Au Bois E.6.a.7.8	26/03/1918	31/03/1918
Heading	31st Divisional Engineers 211st Field Company R.E. April 1918		
Heading	War Diary Of 211th Field Company. R.E. From April 1st To April 30th. 1918 Volume XXVIII		
War Diary	St Amant	01/04/1918	01/04/1918
War Diary	Sus St Leger	02/04/1918	02/04/1918
War Diary	Marquay	03/04/1918	10/04/1918
War Diary	Vieux. Berquin	11/04/1918	12/04/1918
War Diary	Hondeghem	13/04/1918	19/04/1918
War Diary	Le Tir Anglais	20/04/1918	27/04/1918
War Diary	Les Ciseaux.	28/04/1918	30/04/1918
Heading	War Diary Of 211th Field Company. R.E. From 1/5/18 To 31/5/18 Volume XXIX		
War Diary	Les Ciseaux	01/05/1918	23/05/1918
War Diary	Heuringhem	24/05/1918	31/05/1918
Heading	War Diary Of The 211th Field Company R.E. From 1st June 1918 To 30th June 1918 Volume XXX (Original)		
War Diary	Heuringhem	01/06/1918	15/06/1918
War Diary	U.17.6.7.8	16/06/1918	17/06/1918
War Diary	Racquinghem	18/06/1918	20/06/1918
War Diary	C.6.a. 11	21/06/1918	21/06/1918
War Diary	D.9.c.6.3	22/06/1918	30/06/1918
Heading	War Diary Of 211th Field Company R.E. From 1st July 1918 To 31st July 1918 Volume XXXI (Original)		
War Diary	D9c63 Sheet 36A	01/07/1918	31/07/1918
Heading	War Diary Of 211th Field Company R.E. From August 1st To August 31st 1918 Volume XXII (Original)		
War Diary	Transport V.25.c.9.7. (Sheet. 27) Forward D.9.c.6.4. (Sheet 36a)	01/08/1918	31/08/1918
Heading	War Diary of 211th Field Company. R.E. From 1st Sept. to 30th Sept. 1918 Volume XXXIII		
War Diary	La Besace Farm X.9.a.4.4. Sheet 27.S.E.	01/09/1918	01/09/1918
War Diary	Field At 5.27.c.8.6. Sheet 26.S.W)	05/09/1918	22/09/1918
War Diary	Caestre	22/09/1918	28/09/1918
War Diary	S.27.c.8.6	29/09/1918	30/09/1918
Heading	War Diary Of The 211th Field Company R.E. From October 1st To October 31st 1918 Original (Volume XXXIV)		

War Diary	Bailleul	01/10/1918	04/10/1918
War Diary	(T.25.a.02.)	04/10/1918	09/10/1918
War Diary	Bailleul T.25.a.0.2	10/10/1918	16/10/1918
War Diary	Ploegsteert T. 29.d.9.3	17/10/1918	17/10/1918
War Diary	Quesnoy	18/10/1918	19/10/1918
War Diary	Wasquehal	20/10/1918	20/10/1918
War Diary	Freshoy	21/10/1918	24/10/1918
War Diary	Couerhe	25/10/1918	26/10/1918
War Diary	Harlebeke	27/10/1918	30/10/1918
War Diary	Vichte	31/10/1918	31/10/1918
Heading	War Diary Of 211th Field Company. R.E. From 1/11/18 To 30/11/18 Volume XXXV		
War Diary	Vichte	01/11/1918	02/11/1918
War Diary	Vichte & Halluin	03/11/1918	03/11/1918
War Diary	Halluin	04/11/1918	08/11/1918
War Diary	Sweveghem	09/11/1918	09/11/1918
War Diary	Avelghem	10/11/1918	10/11/1918
War Diary	Rehaix	11/11/1918	19/11/1918
War Diary	Rehaix-Khokke	20/11/1918	20/11/1918
War Diary	Khokke-Lauwe	21/11/1918	21/11/1918
War Diary	Lauwe	22/11/1918	24/11/1918
War Diary	Lauwe-Menin	25/11/1918	25/11/1918
War Diary	Menin-Ypres	26/11/1918	26/11/1918
War Diary	Ypres-Steenvoorde	27/11/1918	27/11/1918
War Diary	Steenvoorde-Staple	28/11/1918	28/11/1918
War Diary	Staple St Omer	29/11/1918	29/11/1918
War Diary	St Omer	30/11/1918	30/11/1918
Heading	War Diary Of 211th Field Company R.E. From 1/12/18 to 31/12/18. Volume XXXIV Original		
War Diary	St Omer	01/12/1918	31/12/1918
Heading	War Diary of the 211th. Field Company R.E. for the month of January 1919. Volume XXXVII		
War Diary	St Omer	01/01/1919	31/01/1919
Heading	War Diary 211th Field Company Royal Engineers. February, 1919		
War Diary	St Omer	01/02/1919	28/02/1919
War Diary	St. Omer	01/03/1919	01/03/1919
War Diary	St. Omer	01/04/1919	30/04/1919

31ST DIVISION
DIVL ENGINEERS

211TH FIELD COY R.E.
MAR 1916 – APR 1919

31/211 Field Coy
Vol 1

CONFIDENTIAL

War Diary
of
211th Field Company R.E.

from 1.3.16 to 31.3.16

Apr 19

Army Form C. 2118.

WAR DIARY
or
INTELLIGENCE SUMMARY. 211th Field Company R.E.

(Erase heading not required.)

Instructions regarding War Diaries and Intelligence Summaries are contained in F. S. Regs., Part II. and the Staff Manual respectively. Title pages will be prepared in manuscript.

Place	Date	Hour	Summary of Events and Information	Remarks and references to Appendices
KANTARA (EGYPT)	28/3/16	6.00	Advance party 2 Sergts + 20 other ranks (mounted) entrained for PORT SAID, for Entrainkation to FRANCE.	
KANTARA	1/3/16	5.30	Remainder of Company entrained for PORT SAID.	
		6.10	Detrained & Embarked on S.S. MINNEAPOLIS.	
		19.00	Ship sailed.	
MARSEILLE	6/3/16	13.00	Arrived off MARSEILLES.	
		17.00	Went alongside quay.	
" "	7/3/16	11.00	Disembarked and entrained, leaving station at 14.15	
PONT REMY	9/3/16	13.10	Arrived and detrained. Left working party of 2 N.C.O.'s and 10 men at PONT REMY. Remainder of Company marched to HOCQUINCOURT and billeted.	
HOCQUINCOURT	10/3/16		Advance party arrived with horses, mules and wagons	
" "	11/3/16		Sorted out equipment and packed tool carts	
" "	12/3/16		Same work continued. CRE came over from HALLENCOURT and returned there with O.C. to arrange them for two days of horse transport.	
" "	13/3/16		CRE inspected billets, Carpenters under Lieut. MALLINSON commenced work on timekeepers. Remainder of Company went on march and drill. 9.O.C 2 & 3 + 2 & 3 Companies selected ground for training purposes.	
" "	14/3/16		Visit of CRE re subject of map. Lieut WHITAKER went to ABBEVILLE to purchase material for training. Went on gunnery tomorrow, also work on trenches, latrines etc. in HOCQUINCOURT commenced. Remainder of Company went march and drill. O.C. went found billets for horses for making up strength of Company. C.R. Blah	

Army Form C. 2118.

WAR DIARY
or
INTELLIGENCE SUMMARY.

211th Field Company R.E.

(Erase heading not required.)

Instructions regarding War Diaries and Intelligence Summaries are contained in F.S. Regs., Part II. and the Staff Manual respectively. Title pages will be prepared in manuscript.

Place	Date	Hour	Summary of Events and Information	Remarks and references to Appendices
HOCQUINCOURT	15 9/10		Lieut WHITAKER proceeded to ABBEVILLE with 2 NCOs and 10 men at 2 P.M. material for hutting transport. Returned with material and returned 10 PM	
"	16 9/10 17 9/10		when necessary. Camel drill Rest march Camel drill	
"	18 9/10		Rest march and drill. Guard posted to look out for Aeroplanes. Orders received	
"	19 9/10		for Battn to leave. Lieut. J.B. Whitaker at 5 O.R. went on leave. Visit of G.O.C. Gas helmets given out. Party of Infantry arrived for instruction in mining, and were billeted in HOCQUINCOURT went	
"	20 9/10		to ABBEVILLE to procure spare. Infantry commenced digging shaft south of town at 10 am. note of Lieut Ward went	
"	21 9/10		2/Lt. Wood went to ABBEVILLE with a cart to bring back stores. Infantry commenced mining.	
"	22 9/10		Received orders on subject of mines. Company did drill and practical mining for helmets.	
"	23 9/10		Capt. Hosford and 2 Section Seniors left to do a course of instruction at the bldg. one NCO 3 men went on leave. Company proceeded was of the helmets	
"	24 9/10		Left HOCQUINCOURT at 10 a.m and marched to LONGPRÉ reaching there at 1 p.m. and billeted.	
LONGPRÉ	25 9/10		Left LONGRÉ at 8.0 am and marched to FLESSELLES with 42nd Inf. Bde reaching there at 2 p.m. and billeted.	

Army Form C. 2118.

WAR DIARY
or
INTELLIGENCE SUMMARY. 211th Field Company R.E.

(Erase heading not required.)

Place	Date	Hour	Summary of Events and Information	Remarks and references to Appendices
FLESSELLES	26/3/16		Left FLESSELLES at 8.0 a.m and marched to BEAUVAL with 95th & 7th Ambulances and 222nd Coy A.S.C. reaching there 12. noon, and billeted.	
BEAUVAL	27/3/16		Left BEAUVAL at 9.0 a.m and marched to ENGLEBELMER, reaching there at 4.30 p.m. Was directed to go on to MAILLY-MAILLET and billet there.	
MAILLY MAILLET	28/3/16		Paraded at 10.30 a.m, and marched back to ENGLEBELMER and took over billets of 122nd Fd Coy R.E.. Capt. Hoxton and 2 section serjts rejoined Company. Paraded at 3.30 p.m and put men on to work in billets.	
ENGLEBELMER	29/3/16		Officers went round the trenches, Section Officers with section serjeants and next senior N.C.Os. Lieut Whitaker and 5 other ranks returned from leave. Lieut. put to work on dugouts.	
"	30/3/16		Lieut Whitaker went round to trenches with his section serjt and one other N.C.O. Company at work on dugouts. Capt. Anderson reported to C.R.E. at BUS on the subject of work to be done. Orders received for a move.	
"	31/3/16		Infantry working parties paraded at 8.30 a.m — 2 N.C.O's and 30 men for drainage and cleaning work in communication trenches, 1 officer and 50 men for work on dugouts. Company at work on dugouts. Infantry working party at 9 p.m – 80 men for repairing front line trenches under 2nd Lt Lyon, 20 men under 2nd Lt Wood on dugout for continuance.	

M.C. Anderson
Capt. R.E.

WAR DIARY or INTELLIGENCE SUMMARY

Army Form C. 2118.

211th Field Company R.E.

Place	Date	Hour	Summary of Events and Information	Remarks and references to Appendices
ENGLEBELMER	1.4.16		Infantry working parties paraded at 8.30 a.m. – 2 N.C.O's & 30 men for draining and clearing work in communication trenches. 1 Officer and 50 men for work in the attd. Company at work on dugouts. Infantry working parties at 4 p.m. – 80 men for repairing front line trenches under 2/Lt Flynn). 20 men under 2/Lt. Wood a dug out for cooking.	
" "	2.4.16		Infantry working parties in morning & in a.m. 1.4.16. Parties from Company working at night under 2/Lt Flynn, & West on same work. O.C. & 1/Lt West Riding Field Coy R.E. came over at 3 p.m. and went round trenches with O.C. with a view to taking over.	
" "	3.4.16		Company packed up tool carts in morning. O.C. West Riding Field Coy came into in morning, and went round trenches with O.C. Parks made. 11 Infantrymen paraded at 2 p.m. for work on dugouts. Legatman's letter dated 19th of March ready for move of MARY & & DAY with two 2/Lts. 2nd Lt Routledge and seven men of No 1 Section went out at a.m. when called upon, and dug at some of the 28 men imprisoned by fall of roof. Officer of 1/3 Rear R.E. arrived in afternoon to take over billets and stores.	
" "	4.4.16		Men packed up blankets and sent them off by pontoon wagons to BERTRANCOURT with advanced party. O.C. went round trenches with officers of West Riding R.E. Parties were gone and G.S. wagons loaded in afternoon. Company marched off at 6.30 p.m. reaching BERTRANCOURT at 8 p.m. and went into billets	

Army Form C. 2118.

WAR DIARY
or
INTELLIGENCE SUMMARY.   211th Field Company R.E.

(Erase heading not required.)

Instructions regarding War Diaries and Intelligence Summaries are contained in F.S. Regs., Part II. and the Staff Manual respectively. Title pages will be prepared in manuscript.

Place	Date	Hour	Summary of Events and Information	Remarks and references to Appendices
BERTRAN-COURT	5.4.16		Visit of new C.R.E.. Lieut Malcolm reported at C.R.E's Office at BUS in connection with work with regard to stores. The O.C. went round the village of BERTRANCOURT with the Town Commandant, to see about the water supply.	
"	6.4.16		4 men returned from leave. Work started on 4 incinerators, also the painting of hut roofs and making and painting Motor Lorry notices, O.C. went to see C.R.E. on general business.	
"	7.4.16		Four Infantry working parties commenced work at 8.0 a.m on long communication trench running out from near COLINCAMPS, relieved at 12 noon by parties of the same size. 2.15 pm. in structed party of 100 Infantry in erection of wire entanglements. a JF Wood commenced the erection of a house to be used as a toilet. Other work on 6.4.16 continued.	
"	8.4.16		One man proceeded on special leave. 2 Lt. Epsy and 3 other ranks proceeded on leave, work proceeded on a territorial camp. A party of 12 men went out for night work on making a division of ZAMBUK trench near its junction with HITTITE trench.	
"	9.4.16		Visit of CRE. went out with O.C. to divide sites of dressing station, observation posts and Div. Battle quarters. Wiring parties as before. Work commenced on observation posts. CSM and left the Company, to join a travelling Company, by order of the C.E. VIII Corps. Work continued as before. Horse traffic removed from neighbourhood of BERTRANCOURT and put up by side of any main to avoid for use of inhabitants. Work on divisional stations and Div food periods used for killing horse traffic.	
"	10.4.16		Battle posts commenced. A Company of K.O.Y.L.I attached to Company	
"	11.4.16		Work proceeded as a previous day. A party of men sent out to collect material in the neighbourhood of COLINCAMPS.	

WAR DIARY
INTELLIGENCE SUMMARY

Army Form C. 2118.

211th Field Company R.E.

Place	Date	Hour	Summary of Events and Information	Remarks and references to Appendices
BERTRAN-COURT	12.4.16		Two Infantry working parties owing to Brigade's shortage round. Work on observational posts and general stocks continued, also work done on traverses in EXEEMA trench. A party was out selecting material. A party was out at night (partly R.E.) and partly Pioneers — under "F" W.G.K. on dug out for observation posts.	
"	13.4.16		Work continued as on 12.4.16. Infantry working parties again working on communication trenches. Also on other party a dressing station dug out in COLINCAMPS.	
"	14.4.16		Work as on day before.	
"	15.4.16		Work commenced on putting up tents in huts in COLINCAMPS. Other work continued as before. 1 Sapper and 10 drivers joined the Company from railway.	
"	16.4.16		Work continued. Infantry working parties working near trenches, but no night work instead of day work. Two parties have been out to determine on ELLIS SQUARE and FORT HOMESTEAD. Remainder on digging of new communication trench.	
"	17.4.16		Work as on 16.4.16. A N.C.O.'s and 5 men of searchlight party from Company sent to No 2 Base Reserve Depot, in consequence of recent army order. At about 10 P.m. two men were wounded slightly and one man was injured slightly by a wagon passing. All likely…	

WAR DIARY
INTELLIGENCE SUMMARY. 211th Field Company R.E.

Army Form C. 2118.

Place	Date	Hour	Summary of Events and Information	Remarks and references to Appendices
BERTRANCOURT	17.4.16 contd.		and 7 horses were wounded by shell fire at the same time, one having to be destroyed. This happened while offloading material behind the support line near WATERLOO BRIDGE.	
"	18.4.16		Work continued on painting huts, putting tarred felt onto huts, making notice boards, repairing wells, constructing dug-outs and digging and clearing communication trenches. 2 men returned from leave.	
"	19.4.16		2/Lt. Irving and one man returned from leave, having been delayed on his journey. Work continued on day shift, and work commenced on trenches tools store for Div. Bombing Officer. Also making nets of wire netting and grass to cover dugouts while working on them.	
"	20.4.16		Work as on day before. Also repairs to wells in BERTRANCOURT and fan post damaged by O.P's waggon. Work commenced on wire enclosure for German Prisoners.	
"	21.4.16		150 Infantry on making wire screens. 100 on enclosure for prisoners. 50 on trench stores. 20 on dugouts for A.P.M. 50 on L. RFA observation posts. 50 on Dressing stations. KOYLI on Div battle quarters and dressing stations. 15 RE and 20 KOYLI on O.P's by day. 12 RE and 20 Div cyclists on O.P's by night. 2 reliefs of 150 infantry on completing new communication trench by night. Work in BERTRANCOURT as before.	
"	22.4.16		Work as a day before except that Infantry working parties of 150 did not work at night. New communication trench nearly finished, nearly impossible dry owing to weather. Instead two parties 50 commenced working in Brigade battle quarters.	

WAR DIARY

INTELLIGENCE SUMMARY.

Army Form C. 2118.

211th Field Company
R.E.

Instructions regarding War Diaries and Intelligence Summaries are contained in F.S. Regs., Part II and the Staff Manual respectively. Title pages will be prepared in manuscript.

(Erase heading not required.)

Place	Date	Hour	Summary of Events and Information	Remarks and references to Appendices
BERTRAN- COURT.	23.4.16		Work continued as on 22.4.16	
"	24.4.16		Work as on 23.4.16. Iron pipes collected from SUCRERIE for making BANGALORE torpedoes. CRE went round work with O.C.	
"	25.4.16		Visit of CRE 4th Div. on question of huts. Work on as diary before. Also two reliefs of 100 infantry on clearing PALESTINE and two of 100 on clearing JERICHO. Also 25 making Friday traverses in EXCEMA. 7/8 Bangalore torpedoes made and filled. 3 men forwarded in Depot.	
"	26.4.16		Work proceeded with as diary before. Also parties kept on to clearing PALESTINE and JERICHO trenches. Working Cement sheet to be on floor of trenches	
"	27.4.16		Work on as diary before. Night work started on a new tunnel to join up R.M.C. and 3rd ENTRANCE	
"	28.4.16		Two infantry working parties going to the Brigades changing round. Consequently no work on clear up trenches also.	
"	29.4.16		Work gone on with as on 27.4.16. Also parties put on to clearing up FORT BAILS and FORT HOMSTED.	
"	30.4.16		Work continued on as diary before.	

A. Anderson
Capt. R.E.

Army Form C. 2118.

WAR DIARY
INTELLIGENCE SUMMARY.
(Erase heading not required.)

2/1st Field Company
R.E.
Vol 3

Place	Date	Hour	Summary of Events and Information	Remarks and references to Appendices
BERTRANCOURT	1.5.16		Work continued & repairs to house for stables – Making dug-outs for butts – Making stables – dug-outs at EUSTON DUMP and COLINCAMPS – Bomb stores and other dug-outs at COLINCAMPS – Observation posts in ELLES, TAUPIN, JERICHO, WAGRAM and PYLON. – Clearing of PALESTINE, JERICHO and ZAMBUK. – Repairing PORT ELLES and HOYSTED. – Brigade battle quarters near EXCEMA. Two men wounded by H.E. shell fire, one very severely and died shortly after, the other only slightly, and was admitted to hospital.	
"	2.5.16		150 men of "PERMAMENT WORKING PARTY" put on to clearing out water and of EXCEMA, JEREMIAH, and maintaining dumps. Other work on ditto. 3 men proceeded on leave.	
"	3.5.16		300 men of Permanent working party continued work on same line. Other work on ditto. 150 men put on to clearing SACKVILLE STREET. Lieut. G.B. WHITAKER severely wounded in left hand, and admitted to hospital.	
"	4.5.16		1 man proceeded on leave. Work continued on as on day before.	
"	5.5.16		Work as on day before.	
"	6.5.16		Owing to Brigade changing found no infantry working parties, except Permanent working Party. Work continued on EXCEMA and JEREMIAH, also on OPS, ELLE SQUARE, HOYSTED and SUBABAIB.	

Army Form C. 2118.

WAR DIARY
or
INTELLIGENCE SUMMARY.
(Erase heading not required.)

2/1st Welsh Field Company
R.E.

Place	Date	Hour	Summary of Events and Information	Remarks and references to Appendices
BEATRAN-COURT.	7.5.16		Work continued on deepening EXCEMA, JEREMIAH, SACKVILLE ST, TAUPIN and PYLON, clearing PALESTINE, and various of trench for Decauville railway, dressing station at EUSTON and COLINCAMPS, bomb stores and A.P.M's dugouts, O.P's and Survey Post, concrete defence work at SUCRERIE, marking of cement slabs, construction of huts in BEATRANCOURT and repairs of house. Also digging new C.T. to join up 2nd and 3rd ENTRANCE.	
" "	8.5.16		Deepening of EXCEMA and JEREMIAH being continued. Permanent working party put on to deepening north end of HITTITE and COLCHESTER CAMP on trees on PALESTINE. Other work continued as before.	
" "	9.5.16		Work as on day before. One man proceeded on special leave. Work commenced on forwarding up firewood in ROMAN ROAD. Work out and also in EXCEMA and TAUPIN.	
" "	10.5.16		One man proceeded on special leave. Work as on day before. 2nd Lieut. G.R. Stevens joined the Company, from the Base.	
" "	11.5.16		Permanent working party put on to clearing eastern side of long C.T. running from COLINCAMPS to PYLON road. Casting of Decauville rails commenced. Other work as before.	

Army Form C. 2118.

Instructions regarding War Diaries and Intelligence Summaries are contained in F. S. Regs., Part II. and the Staff Manual respectively. Title pages will be prepared in manuscript.

WAR DIARY
or
INTELLIGENCE SUMMARY.
(Erase heading not required.)

211th Field Company R.E.

Place	Date	Hour	Summary of Events and Information	Remarks and references to Appendices
BERTRAN-COURT	12.5.16		Work commenced on clearing storm of new C.T. from the AVENUE to WATERLOO bridge, and making stopped exits from it. Other work on strong laying of Decauville line commenced by a party of K.O.Y.L.I.	
"	13.5.16		Work as on day before. Permanent working party put on to making traverses at west end of JERICHO.	
"	14.5.16		Two Infantry working parties of army kind. Permanent parties changing round. Work continued on traversing and deepening TAUPIN, a Sunray P.R. and O.P's, dugouts, defence of SUCRERIE, and making FORT ELLIS and HOYSTED	
"	15.5.16		New permanent working party put on to traversing JERICHO, clearing C.T. leading to JERICHO, and digging new trench for Decauville railway, leading to EUSTON DUMP. Other work continued as before.	
"	16.5.16		O.C. went round firetrench from southern limit of Division to SERRE road. Work also continued on permitting timber work into dugouts, and in the SUCRERIE. Remainder of the Company, KOYLI and permanent working party commenced night work on firetrench — making firesteps, and building up traverses.	
"	17.5.16		Work as on 16.5.16	
"	18.5.16		Work as on day before, except for another small party working at putting up PYLON trench	

WAR DIARY or INTELLIGENCE SUMMARY.

Army Form C. 2118.

211th Field Company R.E.

Place	Date	Hour	Summary of Events and Information	Remarks and references to Appendices
BERTRAN-COURT	19.5.16		Work continued on retaining trench, half permanent working party working by day, remainder of men available working by night. Work continued on dugouts at SUCRERIE.	
"	20.5.16		Work as on day before, also 4 R.E. put on to survey post again.	
"	21.5.16		Owing to orders received from CRE, work on fire trench stopped. Work continued on SUCRERIE, survey post and dugouts. One man proceeded on leave.	
"	22.5.16		G.S.O.1, C.R.E. and O.C. visited LA SIGNY FARM in the morning, to consider the preparation of a strong point there. 2Lt. Wood and ½ No. 2 Section working by day with an Infantry battalion, preparing HITTITE, EYCEMA, and perhaps TAUPIN for defence. 2Lt. Lyon and ½ No. 2 Section working at night with a battalion on preparing TAUPIN, FORT BLISS, VIEW, FORT HUYSTED and crescent trench for defence. Work continued on SUCRERIE and permanent survey posts. 2 Sections of 8 company with KOYLI and permanent working parties commenced work at LA SIGNY FARM. Work delayed for an hour, owing to German Artillery.	
"	23.5.16		Work as on day before. Work continued at LA SIGNY farm in erecting wire entanglement, and clearing small gun trenches and a C.T. round the entrance. Infantry did not turn up for work on HITTITE. Owing to orders changing round...	

WAR DIARY
or
INTELLIGENCE SUMMARY.

Army Form C. 2118.

211th Field Company R.E.

Place	Date	Hour	Summary of Events and Information	Remarks and references to Appendices
BERTRANCOURT	24.5.16		No Infantry fatigue for work on HITTITE, EXCEMA, TAUPIN etc. Work on LA SIGNY farm, SUCRERIE and survey post continued.	
"	25.5.16		Infantry resumed work on HITTITE etc. Other work as before.	
"	26.5.16		Holiday order of G.O.C. 8th division. SUCRERIE and survey post. Other work stopped. Work as on day before.	
"	27.5.16		Work as on day before.	
"	28.5.16		Holiday ordered by G.O.C. Work continued on SUCRERIE and survey post.	
"	29.5.16		Work continued on LA SIGNY farm, SUCRERIE and survey post. Work recommenced on O.P's, railway line, trench for railway line, clearance of C.T's, and dressing station dugouts.	
"	30.5.16		Work continued as on day before.	
"	31.5.16		Visit of O.C. to near ALBERT, to see experiments in driving pipes through or into the ground by a hydraulic ram, with a view to using them subsequently to hold explosives for demolition purposes, and for telephone wires. Work proceeded as on day before.	

W.C. Anderson
Captain R.E.
Cmdg 211th Fd Coy R.E.

D.A.G., 3rd Echelon
The Base

Herewith a copy of the War Diary of
the 211th Field Company R.E. for the
month of June.

W A Anderson
Capt R.E.
12.7.16   Comdg 211th Fd Cy R.E.

WAR DIARY
INTELLIGENCE SUMMARY

211th Field Company R.E.

Vol 4

XXXI June

Army Form C. 2118.

Place	Date	Hour	Summary of Events and Information	Remarks and references to Appendices
BERTRANCOURT	1.6.16		24 Wood and one man proceeded on leave. Work was continued by Company, Company of R.W.K. (Pioneers) and permanent working party on Dug and RFA OP's, on north defence work at SUCRERIE, deep dugout for sunken post, footpaths of LA SIGNY farm for defence, laying of Decauville line, preparation of track for the line, and clearing of C.T's.	
"	2.6.16		Work as a day before. Also Infantry parties working on netting & wiring TAUPIN. Parties on clearing long CT's from COLINCAMPS. Work commenced on widen dumps. Rantoon sapper caught by shell fire on BETHUNE COLINCAMPS - COURCELLES road, and 3 mules wounded.	
"	3.6.16		Work as a day before, also work on clearing & draining SOUTHERN trench.	
"	4.6.16		Work proceeded on leave. Work continued as a day before. Work resumed on Brigade Battle quarters near junction of EXCEMA and TAUPIN.	
"	5.6.16		Work as a day before. Infantry party put on to digging a trench along the road, from EUSTON to the medical dugouts south of it. Work very much hindered by rain.	
"	6.6.16		Seventh work at the SUCRERIE completed. Other work as before.	
"	7.6.16		2 men proceeded on leave. Work continued as a day before. One man wounded in left hand by bullet from M.G. fired at one of our aeroplanes.	
"	8.6.16		Work as before.	
"	9.6.16		Work as a day before.	
"	10.6.16		Received orders for the Company to move to COURCELLES. Continued work as a day before, except defence work at LA SIGNY farm. Digging of deep dugouts commenced by R.W.K. Infantry at KOYLI at battery position under R.E. supervision.	

Army Form C. 2118.

WAR DIARY
or
INTELLIGENCE SUMMARY. 211th Field Company R.E.

(Erase heading not required.)

Instructions regarding War Diaries and Intelligence Summaries are contained in F. S. Regs., Part II. and the Staff Manual respectively. Title pages will be prepared in manuscript.

Place	Date	Hour	Summary of Events and Information	Remarks and references to Appendices
BERTRANCOURT	11.6.16		Company marched to COURCELLES and billeted there. No R.E. work found for working parties. Work continued on deep dugouts, O.P.'s, ration dumps, laying of trench railway, brigade battle quarters, survey post dugout, trench from EUSTON to dugouts and maintenance of trenches.	
COURCELLES	12.6.16		No. 4 Section moved out to EUSTON dugouts, and commenced maintenance work in the front line South of the SERRE road. Work continued as in day before. 2 men proceeded on leave.	
" "	13.6.16		Work as in day before.	
" "	14.6.16		Work as in day before.	
" "	15.6.16		Survey post in ELLES SQUARE completed. Work continued as before. Dugouts started partway on the clearing NORTHERN CENTRAL and RAILWAY trench, on to the PYLON road.	
" "	16.6.16		Work as before. Work commenced on telephone stores in TAUPIN. Also on dugouts for M.P.L. COLINCAMPS. 3 Pylons in line of fire of Artillery pulled down. A bridge put across road at EUSTON.	
" "	17.6.16		Work on O.P.'s, battle quarters ration dumps, dugouts, railway, and clearing of trench continued. 168 Infantry fort into clearing SACKVILLE St. north of RED COTTAGE.	
" "	18.6.16		Work as before. Also work on construction of railway trucks for Decauville line. Ration dumps completed. One man wounded in the head by a piece of shrapnel shell.	
" "	19.6.16		Work as before. Also placing of manure boards in trenches, repairs to work in COURCELLES and filling up of gaps in hedge, running inside TAUPIN with branches (ELLESSQUARE UP completed)	
" "	20.6.16		Brigade battle quarters completed. Other work continued.	
" "	21.6.16		Work continued as before. Digging of shelter trenches for the Company in COURCELLES commenced.	

WAR DIARY
or
INTELLIGENCE SUMMARY

Army Form C. 2118.

2/1st Field Company
R.E.

Place	Date	Hour	Summary of Events and Information	Remarks and references to Appendices
COURCELLES	22.6.16		Work continued on deep dugouts, Bn.O.P in WAGRAM, R.F.A. O.P's in PYLON, clearing of SACKVILLE & laying of railway line, shelters for runners near Brigade battle quarters, and construction of trucks. Work on a O.P's and dam of railway trucks.	
" "	23.4.16			
" "	24.6.16		Bombardment commenced. One Officer and 6 men went to VARENNES to practise the erection and dismantling of Inglis bridge. Remainder of Company practised rapid wiring.	
" "	25.6.16		One Officer and 6 men went to VARENNES. Remainder of Company practised rapid wiring entanglements. Portable road bridge constructed.	
" "	26.6.16		One Officer and 6 men went to VARENNES. Party sent out to knife water out of C.T's. Remainder of Company trained in COURCELLES. COURCELLES shelled. One man wounded. Bridge taken out at night and carried to WATERLOO BRIDGE. Two men of this party wounded.	
" "	27.6.16		A party out pumping water out of C.T's. 2 men sent out to repair Decauville line when it had been hit by a shell. Remainder of Company practising wiring.	
" "	28.6.16		Party out pumping water out of C.T's. Remainder of Company practising wiring.	
" "	29.6.16		O party at pumping, remainder reconnoitering Héros trench etc. Remainder probably wiring. Carpenters out and attempts to fix a table in a watermain to see if water could be pumped in it. A bridge constructed and taken out to OBSERVATION WOOD. Company practised wiring at night. One man wounded. One officer pulled down by wind.	

SECRET

Vol 5

<u>Confidential</u>

War Diary

of

<u>211th Fld. Coy R.E.</u>

<u>July 1st to July 31st, 1916.</u>

Volume <u>VII</u>

<u>Confidential</u>

Army Form C. 2118.

WAR DIARY
or
INTELLIGENCE SUMMARY.

211th Field Company R.E.

(Erase heading not required.)

Instructions regarding War Diaries and Intelligence Summaries are contained in F.S. Regs., Part II and the Staff Manual respectively. Title pages will be prepared in manuscript.

Place	Date	Hour	Summary of Events and Information	Remarks and references to Appendices
COURCELLES	1.7.16		Attack commenced 7.30 a.m. 2 portable bridges constructed. Company remained at Courcelles awaiting orders. Owing to the progress of the attack no further work at night.	
" "	2.7.16		Four sections of Company sent to clear the forward ends of NORTHERN CENTRAL RAILWAY and SOUTHERN trenches.	
" "	3.7.16		3 sections out by day clearing CT's up to and the front line trenches by front. 2 sections went out at night under 2/Lt STEVENS to do wiring of front line trenches.	
" "	4.7.16		Orders received for a move. Two working parties sent out, one in connection with HOSPITAL and the interpreter sent on to BUS, to arrange for billets.	
" "	5.7.16		Company paraded at 1 p.m. and moved to BUS, going into billets there.	
BUS	6.7.16		Company paraded at 7 a.m. and marched to the outskirts of LOUVENCOURT and from there to BEAUVAL, reaching BUS at 1.20 p.m. and went into billets.	
BEAUVAL	7.7.16		Company paraded at 7 a.m. and marched to CANDAS, reaching there at 9 a.m. and went into billets. Orders received to move.	
CANDAS	8.7.16		Tool carts and party on wagons packed again. 2 C. went on to CONTEVILLE to reconnoitre the route there. Company paraded at 11 p.m. and marched to CONTEVILLE station, and reached DOMLEGER at 3 a.m.	
CONTEVILLE	9.7.16		Train arrived very late at 5.15. The company was entrained by 7.30 a.m. Train left at 9.50 a.m. Arrived at BERGUETTE station at 1.30 p.m. and detrained. Company fell in at 3 p.m. after having dinners, and marched to BURNES reaching there at 5.30 p.m. and went into billets.	
BURNES	10.7.16		Company did small details, and 2 Sect. cart men on stoppering and cleaning of horses and carts.	

Army Form C. 2118.

WAR DIARY
or
INTELLIGENCE SUMMARY.
(Erase heading not required.)

Instructions regarding War Diaries and Intelligence Summaries are contained in F. S. Regs, Part II and the Staff Manual respectively. Title pages will be prepared in manuscript.

211th Field Company
R.E.

Place	Date	Hour	Summary of Events and Information	Remarks and references to Appendices
BUSNES	11.7.16		Company cleaning up and drill. Two prisoners taken after the CRE at ST VENANT. Squad drill in morning, kit inspection in afternoon.	
" "	12.7.16		Company cleaning up carts for inspection by G.O.C. Army. Officers arrived at 9.30 Brigade HQ, BUSNES for lecture by G.O.C. Corps.	
" "	13.7.16			
" "	14.7.16		Warning received at 2.a.m. that Division was to move. Orders received at 2.30 p.m. that inspection by G.O.C. Army was postponed. ~~but that Busnes by 1.30 p.m.~~ ~~West of LESTREM~~ ~~Here at 4.30 p.m. and billeted there.~~ Company paraded at 2 p.m. and marched to BUSNETTE, to fill up two holes in a field there.	
L'EPINETTE " "	15.7.16		Marching orders received saying that Company was to leave BUSNES at 1.30 p.m. Paraded at 1.30 p.m. and marched to L'EPINETTE, west of LESTREM, reaching there at 4.30 p.m. and billeted there.	
L'EPINETTE	16.7.16		The Company washed their clothes. Capt Horspool and the Interpreter went to BOUT DEVILLE and RIEZ BAILLEUL to see advance billets there. O.C. went to see CRE at LESTREM in the evening, and received orders to move to BOUT DEVILLE.	
L'EPINETTE	17.7.16		Capt Horspool, 2nd Lt. GUY and the advance left for BOUT DEVILLE at 6 a.m to obtain billets. Company paraded at 10.45 a.m. and marched to BOUT DEVILLE there at 12.30 p.m. and billeted there.	

WAR DIARY

INTELLIGENCE SUMMARY.

Army Form C. 2118.

211th Field Company
R.E.

(Erase heading not required.)

Place	Date	Hour	Summary of Events and Information	Remarks and references to Appendices
LEPINETTE BOUT DEVILLE	18.7.16		Sergt Rean and Pioneer Morris appeared before a Court Martial in charge of drunkeness. Capt Hawkpool and 2nd Lt Wood among the witnesses. Sergt Rean found "not guilty", O.C. and 2nd Lt Eyny went round the trenches. Company numbers 1 - 53 & MAISONS for a bath. O.C. went to H.Q. 142nd Infantry Brigade at LAVENTIE in the afternoon. Capt Hampool, 2nd Lt Eyny and 2nd Lt Stevens sent out at night supervising Infantry working parties, working in accordance with the support line.	
"	19.7.16		Two usual in trenches during day, owing to an attack being made by Australians and 61st Division in north of 31st Division's front. Infantry were to L'EPINETTE FM under Lt Mullinson to make frames for sally ports, 2nd Lt Eyny and Stevens sent with 40 men to mine sally port through frame line thereabout, but carrying party of 50 Infantry at L'EPINETTE FM. Carrying party were taken away, as reinforcements would normally have made the stand by. No work carried out.	
"	20.7.16		Lt Mullinson was working by day, when party of 15 an repairing to support line WINCHESTER trench, O.C. and 2nd Lt Wood went round. Names of support trenches reported state of it to Brigadier. 2nd Lts. Eyny and Stevens sent at night in afternoon sinning an 4 sally ports.	
"	21.7.16		Lt Mullinson with 35 men working by day on Reserve line, south of ERITH trench. Also 30 Infantry working on north of ERITH trench. And another 10 at night Elaborators at L'EPINETTE FM in morning making frames for building from 2nd Lts Eyny and Stevens with 40 men in sally ports in afternoon and evening.	

Army Form C. 2118.

WAR DIARY
or
INTELLIGENCE SUMMARY. 211½ Field Company R.E.
(Erase heading not required.)

Instructions regarding War Diaries and Intelligence Summaries are contained in F. S. Regs., Part II. and the Staff Manual respectively. Title pages will be prepared in manuscript.

Place	Date	Hour	Summary of Events and Information	Remarks and references to Appendices
BOUT DEVILLE	22.7.16		Lt. Mewlinson with party of 32 worked on Reserve line. Also Infantry on an previous day. Lt. Eyre inspected BATH trench west of front line, which in view to its repair. 2 Lt. Stevens with 28 men working on Saley party. 3 completed, and not quite inspected. 60 Infantry under 2nd Lt. Eyre working at night on repairing BATH trench.	
" "	23.7.16		Message received at 3.15 a.m. that Brigade was being relieved, consequently no work required in trenches. Orders received to move to LACOUTURE.	
" "	24.7.16		Capt. Hearst and proceeded to LACOUTURE to take over billets from the 227th Fd Coy R.E. Lt. Mewlinson and 2nd Lt. Ward and Stevens went round the new area of trenches. Company paraded at 3 p.m. and marched to LACOUTURE, arriving there at 6 p.m. and billeted.	
LACOUTURE	25.7.16		3 Sections of the Company put on work on the Reserve line on North side of CADBURY trench. The fourth to the North were brought down to the other side and to being billeted. The men dictum worked at the R.E. dump at LACOUTURE.	
" "	26.7.16		Two platoons of KOYLI (32 men in each) started working with the Company. Work as on the day before. Party working north of CADBURY again taken back of that trench. 8 men part on to completing 2 RFA O.P's in the RUE DE BOIS. Work on the reserve line south of CADBURY, and on the O.P's.	
" "	27.7.16		Work as on the day before.	
" "	28.7.16			
" "	29.7.16		Work continued on reserve line and O.P's. A road bridge put across a trench running across EDWARD ROAD, on the way to FACTORY CORNER.	

WAR DIARY

INTELLIGENCE SUMMARY. 211th Field Company R.E.

Army Form C. 2118.

Place	Date	Hour	Summary of Events and Information	Remarks and references to Appendices
LACOUTURE	30.7.16		One Platoon of K.O.Y.L.I. and one section of the Company put on to work on the Reserve line north of CADBURY from 4 a.m. to 8 a.m. Remainder working on the post south of CADBURY, on the O.P's, Carpenters went at LACOUTURE and setting out stores. LACOUTURE shelled at night with 5.9 H.E.	
" "	31.7.16		Party did not go out early in the morning. Work done south of CADBURY and on O.P. A few shells in LACOUTURE in the morning. A considerable number of shells in the afternoon. The Company water cart was caught by the first shell, and the water-man severely wounded, dying soon after. Driver wounded. One horse killed outright, the other had to be destroyed. Water cart full of holes	

E.C. Cushman
Capt. R.E.
Comdg 211th F. Coy R.E.

Vol 6

CONFIDENTIAL

War Diary
of
211th Field Company R.E.

from 1.8.16. to 31.8.16
(Volume VIII).

WAR DIARY

INTELLIGENCE SUMMARY. 211th Field Company R.E.

Army Form C. 2118.

(Erase heading not required.)

Place	Date	Hour	Summary of Events and Information	Remarks and references to Appendices
LACOUTURE	1.8.16		One Section of the Company and 30 K.O.Y.L.I. working on the "B" Line north of CADBURY from 4 a.m. to 8 a.m. during mist. One R.E. wounded by shell fire. One Section working south of CADBURY, reconstructing B Line from 2 p.m. assisted by 20 Infantry, and 20 men all electing and knocking bricks. One section working on same path from 2 p.m. to 8 p.m., with 30 K.O.Y.L.I. and 40 Infantry as before.	
" "	2.8.16		No mist in the early morning, so that the path was put into order as those south of CADBURY. Other work continued as before.	
" "	3.8.16		Still no mist. Work continued as on 2.8.16. Lacouture shelled in the evening without about 12 77 m.m. shells.	
" "	4.8.16		Work continued as a day before.	
" "	5.8.16		Work as on day before.	
" "	6.8.16		Work gone on with on OLD British line north of CADBURY. Other work as on day before.	
" "	7.8.16		Section continued work on O.B.L. in early morning. K.O.Y.L.I. delayed arrival and so did not work early but from 8 a.m. to 2 p.m. Officer went as before. Work as on 6.8.16. C.R.E. went round "B" Line with O.C. Company. 5 77 m.m. shells fired into LACOUTURE during evening.	
" "	8.8.16		Party of 200 Infantry went at night in pastro of livestock, munitions from BOURNVILLE to B.S.L north of CADBURY falling in barrel. Work not completed.	

Army Form C. 2118.

Army Form C. 2118.

WAR DIARY
or
INTELLIGENCE SUMMARY.
(Erase heading not required.)

211th Field Company
R.E.

Instructions regarding War Diaries and Intelligence Summaries are contained in F. S. Regs., Part II. and the Staff Manual respectively. Title pages will be prepared in manuscript.

Place	Date	Hour	Summary of Events and Information	Remarks and references to Appendices
LACOUTURE	9.8.16		One section and party of Coy. LI working on O.B.L. in early morning. Work continued on BOURNVILLE Infrastructure(?).	
"	10.8.16		One section and a party of infantry put on to work strengthening a short piece of front line just north of QUINQUE RUE. Other work as before.	
"	11.8.16		Work on 10.8.16. LACOUTURE shelled during afternoon and evening with 77 m.m. and later with 5.9".	
"	12.8.16		Work as before except that Coy LI party working on BOURNVILLE were moved to work on O.B.L. south of RUPE trench.	
"	13.8.16		Work as before. Also work done on drainage station dugout in KING'S ROAD, sand-bags work in dugout at TUBE STATION for T.M. (Bay), and putting up tank for water supply in LACOUTURE.	
"	14.8.16		Work as before.	
"	15.8.16		Section of Company working on BOURNVILLE moved to O.B.L. south of RUPE. A Canvas screen put up at night across the CINDER TRACK, at the gap in the Quesne(?) tin(?).	
"	16.8.16		Work as on 15.8.16. A few 77 m.m. shells fired into LACOUTURE during the afternoon.	
"	17.8.16		Work as on dany before.	
"	19.8.16		Work as on dany before.	

2353 Wt. W2544/1454 700,000 5/15 D.D.&L. A.D.S.S./Forms/C. 2118.

WAR DIARY
INTELLIGENCE SUMMARY.
(Erase heading not required.)

Army Form C. 2118.

211th Field Company R.E.

Place	Date	Hour	Summary of Events and Information	Remarks and references to Appendices
LACOUTURE	19.8.16		One man killed while working on "B" line in the morning. Work as on day before.	
" "	20.8.16		Work continued as on day before.	
" "	21.8.16		Work commenced on facing bridges and ditches on extreme side of CINDER TRACK near "B" Line. Other work as before.	
" "	22.8.16		Work as before. A few shells put in to LACOUTURE in the afternoon.	
" "	23.8.16		Work as before.	
" "	24.8.16		Some work done in mending O.B.L. south of BOND STREET. Other work continued.	
" "	25.8.16		Work as on 24.8.16. Revetment work put up at gap in "B" line at CINDER TRACK. LACOUTURE shelled during the early morning, afternoon and night.	
" "	26.8.16		Work continued as on 25.8.16. ‡ LACOUTURE shelled in the evening.	
" "	27.8.16		Work as on day before. LACOUTURE shelled in early morning.	
" "	28.8.16		A sapper received injuries to his left hand on the circular saw. Work on O.B.L. stopped for the day. Work was done instead on parade of GUARDS trench. Other work continued.	
" "	29.8.16		Work done on O.B.L. south of ROPE, north of CADBURY, south of BOND ST., On GUARDS trench and on the gap at the CINDER TRACK. 2nd Lt. W.L. Egany was admitted to hospital sick.	
" "	30.8.16		Some men of the K.O.Y.L.I. put on to making a clearway for tramway extension. Other work as before.	
" "	31.8.16		Work as on day before. One man wounded while returning from work on O.B.L. south of ROPE.	

Confidential

Vol 9

War Diary

211th Field Coy. R.E.

31st Division

September 1916.

WAR DIARY

INTELLIGENCE SUMMARY

Army Form C. 2118.

2/1st Field Company R.E.

Place	Date	Hour	Summary of Events and Information	Remarks and references to Appendices
LACOUTURE	1.9.16		Worked on repairing O.B.L. south of ROPE and north of CADBURY. Making up parapet at CINDER TRACK. Building traverse to GUARDS trench near BOND ST. Broad stone on RUB-U-DUB. Clearing trench for extension of tram line. R.F.A. O.P. at the FACTORY.	
"	2.9.16		Work as on day before. Also a party in the front line strengthening the parapet.	
"	3.9.16		Work as on day before.	
"	4.9.16		No work on O.B.L. north of CADBURY. Other work as before. Lay boards on front line parapet and dugouts.	
"	5.9.16		Work as on 3.9.16. Also parties making up parados of newly built FACTORY trench support. CADBURY, COCKSPUR, BOND ST. and VINE.	
"	6.9.16		Work as on day before.	
"	7.9.16		Work as on day before.	
"	8.9.16		Work as on day before.	
"	9.9.16		Work as on day before. Also a party clearing drains of [illegible] [illegible] cleaning C.T.s and repairing trench boards. Work on a dug out to house station dugout in KING GEORGE'S road. Repairs to roof of Brigade billet broken dug out.	
"	10.9.16		Work as on day before, a few occurred in the Company. N.C.O. and 2 [illegible] was put at Lt. Abm[?]. [illegible] day off on 2 [illegible] came in the afternoon to prepare papers. Yesterday. Also Divisional Claims officer.	
"	11.9.16			
"	12.9.16		Work as on day before. Work commenced on putting permanent roof on KINGS ROAD dressing station O.P.	

WAR DIARY / INTELLIGENCE SUMMARY

Army Form C. 2118.

211th Field Company R.E.

Place	Date	Hour	Summary of Events and Information	Remarks and references to Appendices
LACOUTURE	13.9.16		Work as on day before.	
"	14.9.16		Work as on day before.	
"	15.9.16		Work as on day before, except that parties making up/repairs of G.T.s were cancelled. Lewis gunners told of by fire.	
"	16.9.16		Work as on day before.	
"	17.9.16		2/3rd and 9/4th Brigades moved down to FESTUBERT and GIVENCHY areas. 9/2nd Brigade extended line to LA BASSEE road. Work as on day before. O.C. in rear joined to proceed on leave.	
"	18.9.16		Work as on day before. Work commenced on material WATERS KEEP 25/25. W.T. Egny returned to the Company from hospital.	
"	19.9.16		Work as on day before. Work commenced on new B line & digging trenches on either side of LANSDOWNE and laying floor boards in LA BASSEE road. Also repairing done of OVEN O.P. which had been hit by a shell.	
"	20.9.16		Work as on day before.	
"	21.9.16		Work as on day before.	
"	22.9.16		Work as on day before. Work commenced on R.F.A. O.P.s at SAVOY, BARRICADE HOUSE, THE NOOK & THE MOORHEN.	
"	23.9.16		Work as on day before.	
"	24.9.16		O/C proceeded on leave. Work as on day before. Work commenced on trenches at RICHEBOURG ST VAAST.	
"	25.9.16		Count of Engrs on fire reassembled. Work as on day before. C.S.M. John returned from leave. Lectures and practical instruction work commenced at PACAUT.	
"	26.9.16		Work as day before. Work commenced on "IT".	

Army Form C. 2118.

WAR DIARY

INTELLIGENCE SUMMARY. 211th Field Coy R.E.

(Erase heading not required.)

Place	Date	Hour	Summary of Events and Information	Remarks and references to Appendices
LACOUTRE	27.9.16		Work as day before. "Gas Alert" at 3 p.m. 7H	
"	28.9.16		Work as day before. "Gas Alert" at 3 p.m.	
"	29.9.16		Work as day before. "Gas tent taken off at 2pm. Lt E. Wallwin and 2/. Lt. W L Guy and 6 O.R. attended Flammenwerfer and Bayonet Defence demonstration at Bn School of Instruction PACAUT. PIONEER E Eden No. 83909 proceeded on leave.	
"	30/9/16		Work as day before.	

Hunter Capt RE
OC 211 Field Coy RE

Vol 8

CONFIDENTIAL

War Diary
of
211th Field Company R.E.

from 1.10.16 to 31.10.16

(Volume 10)

Army Form C. 2118.

WAR DIARY
or
INTELLIGENCE SUMMARY.

2nd F.C.A. Coy R.E.

(Erase heading not required.)

Instructions regarding War Diaries and Intelligence Summaries are contained in F.S. Regs., Part II. and the Staff Manual respectively. Title pages will be prepared in manuscript.

Place	Date	Hour	Summary of Events and Information	Remarks and references to Appendices
LACOUTURE	1.10.16		Work as on day before. 2nd Lieut STEVENS R.G. to Hospital.	
" "	2.10.16		Working parties reduced.	
" "	3.10.16		Working parties still further reduced. Reconnd HAWKINSON E. and 2nd Lieut WOOD C.J. (Sappers) four officers & 1/2 HOME COUNTIES Fd Coy R.E. (mining) works.	
" "	4.10.16		Coy preparing to move. One officer and 5 NCOs were of 1/2 HOME COUNTIES F Coy and 5 sappers and work on tunnels joining 2 mining groups met.	
" "	5.10.16		Coy marched off at 2pm and went into billets at CALONNIE-SUR-LA-LYS. 6pm	
CALONNE-SUR-LA-LYS	6.10.16		Coy at rest. Advance party to Railway Card. 2/3 returns forms received.	
" "	7.10.16		Coy did route march. Orders for movement received.	
" "	8.10.16		Packing up carts. Parked tom. at 6pm and marched to MERVILLE and entrained.	
" "	9.10.16		Pontoon wagons ordered at 9am. marched to MERVILLE and entrained. 4 p.m. Pontoons reached YAUCHELLES at 6.30 p.m.	
YAUCHELLES	10.10.16		Put up drover (?) and slung kitchen to round them. We were met at train last Atonpont, 2nd Lt WOOD and Lynn and 4 Section Sergeants and sent train-loaded with main went to VARENNES to be quartered at NISSEY Bay hutes. This day did not have place. In afternoon O.C. and 2nd L WOOD went out to several of billets.	
" "	11.10.16		Part of HOME tench. 300 Infantry were attached a string of eight. Who would take (?) Lt Wood 1 NCO & 6 men went to 60 QUEENS in 30th an OA 30 Eng men until for groceries. 5 men making duckboards at MARIEUX. Body transport of ammunition	
" "	12.10.16		party widening HOME trench.	
" "	13.10.16		Work as on day before. No further work on HOME trench.	

Army Form C. 2118.

WAR DIARY
INTELLIGENCE SUMMARY. 2/1st Field Company R.E.

(Erase heading not required.)

Place	Date	Hour	Summary of Events and Information	Remarks and references to Appendices
VAUCHELLES	14.10.16		No. 2 Section moved out to COURCELLES. A platoon of 9/2nd Bn Staffords instructed in making Strong Point. Work done in repairs to pumps and making troughs at St LEGER. Three limes cleaned ground and levelled off. Work on Broadwires continued. Work continued on horse troughs, and making & greasing. Marking party water carriers commenced.	
"	15.10.16		Repairs to pump in VAUCHELLES. Work commenced on cement work at troughs. Work in troughs and spandaus continued. Orders to move received.	
"	16.10.16		Packed up. Paraded at 10 a.m. and marched to COIGNEUX and billeted there, at the R.E. Dump.	
"	17.10.16			
COIGNEUX	18.10.16		Work continued on troughs at St LEGER. Rest of day cleaning up rifles and arranging stores in Dump.	
"	19.10.16		Work as before.	
"	20.10.16		Repairs to gun loopt steps in HEBUTERNE commenced. Rd. D dump at SAILLY taken over. Work commenced on hut and latrine for ORS at SAILLY. [?] RE & CRE finished the company.	
"	21.10.16		Work commenced on repairs to hut in WARNIMONT WOOD. Also work on latrine. Also a spring in THIEVRES. Work on later.	
"	22.10.16		Work commenced on repairs to dugouts of XIII H.Q at SAILLY. Work done in WARNIMONT WOOD. Other work as before.	
"	23.10.16		Work as on day before.	
"	24.10.16		Commenced making brackets for stretchers, to be put up in dressing station at HEBUTERNE. Other work as before. No 2 3 & 4 sections under R. Pond and 2nd Lt Flying were out at night marking out route from CAGE & tunnel, forward to TOMs trench. Capt [?] went on leave.	

2353 Wt. W2544/1454 700,000 5/15 D.D.&L. A.DSS/Forms/C. 2118.

Army Form C. 2118.

WAR DIARY
INTELLIGENCE SUMMARY. 211th Field Company R.E.

(Erase heading not required.)

Instructions regarding War Diaries and Intelligence Summaries are contained in F. S. Regs., Part II. and the Staff Manual respectively. Title pages will be prepared in manuscript.

Place	Date	Hour	Summary of Events and Information	Remarks and references to Appendices
COIGNEUX	25.10.16		Work commenced on repairs to huts in COUIN wood. Other work on trench repairs to hand at Div. Baths at AUTHIE. Also to tombs at COUIN. Party out at night under 2/Lts POUND and MALLINSON completing making out of works. Work on trench towards commenced	
" "	26.10.16		Work continued in COUIN huts, making trench boards etc.	
" "	27.10.16		Work as on day before. Also making table and sidebaards. A party at putting up of frames.	
" "	28.10.16		Work as on day before.	
" "	29.10.16		Work as on day before.	
" "	30.10.16		Work as on day before. Work commenced on baths at ROSSIGNOL FARM	
" "	31.10.16		Work as on day before. 2nd Lt Wilby wounded & No 3. C.C.S.	

m. G. Gardner
Capt. RE

Confidential

Volume XI

Vol 9

War Diary.

31st Division

211th Field Coy R.E.

November 1916.

WAR DIARY

INTELLIGENCE SUMMARY 211th Field Company R.E.

Army Form C. 2118.

Place	Date	Hour	Summary of Events and Information	Remarks and references to Appendices
COIGNEUX	1.11.16		Work continued on erecting huts at NEWCAMP, COUIN, fixing stretcher rests at dressing station, WARLINCOURT. Repairs to horse troughs at COIGNEUX. Fixing electric light fitting at Div Sounds ORVILLE, putting up drying room at baths, ROSSIGNOL FARM. Repairs to GRAYS' and SAILLY. Broken down hut at Div Baths, AUTHIE. Also making trench tracks. TM emplacements, archways, gypsum huts, horse troughs, notice boards, steam pipes.	
"	2.11.16		Work as on day before.	
"	3.11.16		Work as before. Also having dugout at ADMA 91 hdqrs dusting room and air battery pushed into by Bosch round enfind in Dump. Fixing stove in smith for 75th Fd Amb.	
"	4.11.16		Work as before. Also fixing huts at Div laundry. Constructing table at HENUWOOD FARM. Also strengthening and cleaning 23/Amm dump. Also artillery lookout AUTHIE.	
"	5.11.16		Work as before. Also fixing huts in Cuckoo wood trench with brick partition wall in hut of 95th Fd Amb bathe, COIGNEUX. Mending huts at ... of Ampco hut in BAYENCOURT — BUS road. Making trench tracks.	
"	6.11.16		Work as on day before.	
"	7.11.16		Work as before. New hut at ... COUIN complete, 1 latrine, cookhouse table, 2 forms made. Repairs to roofs of huts in COUIN WOOD. also parties dumps in lathe. Also making huts/bath and seats at ROSSIGNOL FARM baths, and having ... on men's hut.	
"	8.11.16		And man proceeded on leave. Capt Harwood injured from ...2/Lt R.P. Stevens joined the Company to replace 2nd Lt W. Byng (sick). Work as before. Supervision of Div Baths attended to working rooms and recovering dressing rooms.	
"	9.11.16		Work as before. Also erection of horse standings for 92nd Bn Regiment of BAYENCOURT. Repairs to MARK huts SAILLY-AU-BOIS. Repairing water tank in COUIN.	

WAR DIARY

INTELLIGENCE SUMMARY. 211th Field Company R.E.

Army Form C. 2118.

Instructions regarding War Diaries and Intelligence Summaries are contained in F.S. Regs., Part II. and the Staff Manual respectively. Title pages will be prepared in manuscript.

(Erase heading not required.)

Place	Date	Hour	Summary of Events and Information	Remarks and references to Appendices
COIGNEUX	10.11.16		Work on huts at COUIN stopped, and work on erecting Nissen huts at BAYENCOURT–BUS road commenced. Also putting up huts at Dieu Samedi, ORVILLE. Other work as before.	
"	11.11.16		Work as on day before. Also repairs to huts at ROSSIGNOL FARM. Facing roads inside No 46 WELSH SAILLY trenches as a gun-transport station. Also felling and removing two large trees dangerously overhanging horse lines in AUTHIE WOOD.	
"	12.11.16		No 3 & 4 Sections rested during the day. Worked on day before, nothing done in Dump. No 3 & 4 Sections paraded at 5 p.m. and marched up to CABER TRENCH, picking up a pick and shovel apiece on the way. Sections under 2nd Lieut. dePaud and 2nd Lt. Pearson. O.C. went to Brigade Battle Quarters in PAPIN TRENCH.	
"	13.11.16		Attack commenced at 5.45 a.m. No 3 Section ordered forward at 10.30 a.m. to work in strong points. Unable to advance owing to heavy enemy barrage. No 3 & 4 Sections established withdrew from CABER Trench. Were ordered to return to COIGNEUX at 6 p.m. Reached home 9 p.m. Casualties: 1 Sapper killed, 2 N.C.O.s wounded, 2 sappers wounded.	
"	14.11.16		Other work as on day before.	
"	15.11.16		No 3 & 4 Sections resting. Work as on day before. Also putting up small shelters and digging hut at 95 & 79 Ambulance, COIGNEUX. One N.C.O. proceeded on leave.	
"	16.11.16		Work as before. Work recommenced on huts at COUIN WOOD huts.	
"	17.11.16		Work as before.	2nd Lt. Q.G. Stevens admitted to Hospital, sick.
"	18.11.16		Work as before. 16 R.E. and 36 Infantry went out to live in dugouts in PAPIN Trench (K.21. central), for work on deep dug out in DUQUESCOY and JENA. Also sections 10 & 9.3 B.E. have started

Army Form C. 2118.

WAR DIARY
INTELLIGENCE SUMMARY. 211th Field Company R.E.

(Erase heading not required.)

Place	Date	Hour	Summary of Events and Information	Remarks and references to Appendices
COIGNEUX	19.11.16		Work as in diary before. Work on deep dugouts commenced. Also a small party sent out to clear VERCINGETORIX trench.	
"	20.11.16		Work as in diary before. Also marthes, latrines and latrines for horse lines encampment.	
"	21.11.16		Work as in diary before.	
"	22.11.16		Work as in diary before. No. 2 & 4 Sections paraded at 2 p.m. and marched to SAILLY DELL and took over huts there. Work on dugouts in DU QUESNOY and TENA handed over to 210th Fd. Coy. R.E.	
"	23.11.16		Work commenced on cleaning of "R" line north of WARRIOR. By No. 2 section. Work commenced on cleaning YANKEE and YOUNG and SACHA. ROSSIGNOL FARM baths completed. Wrapping straw round waterpipes at AUTHIE completed. Lt. J.M. Stowell joined the company.	
"	24.11.16		Work as in diary before. Work commenced on repairs to Gun Cot. Store at SAILLY. Two men proceeded on leave.	
"	25.11.16		Work continued on cont. trenches, ablution sheds and latrines for Nissen Hut Camp. Fitting of racks in gumboot store completed, repairs to roof commenced. Other work as before. Lt. E. Mucallinson R.E. proceeded on leave.	
"	26.11.16		Work as before. Work done on baths of Officers Mess hut and Mess & Kits of Sergeants Mess hut at COUIN. Hut and cook racks fixed in Div. Baths, AUTHIE.	
"	27.11.16		Work on Nissen huts temporarily stopped and R.E. and Infantry working as Guard on by asphalt 210th Fd. Coy. R.E. on living parties at YELLOW LINE (KELLERMAN and GOLFSBAINS)	

2353 Wt. W2544/1454 700,000 5/15 D. D. & L. A.D.S.S./Forms/C. 2118.

Army Form C. 2118.

WAR DIARY
INTELLIGENCE SUMMARY. 211th Field Company R.E.

(Erase heading not required.)

Instructions regarding War Diaries and Intelligence Summaries are contained in F. S. Regs., Part II and the Staff Manual respectively. Title pages will be prepared in manuscript.

Place	Date	Hour	Summary of Events and Information	Remarks and references to Appendices
COIGNEUX	28.11.16		Work continued as before.	
"	29.11.16		Work as day before. Wire in front of Yellow Line "completed". No men instructing lear.	
"	30.11.16		Wiring party rested during the day. Other work as before. 21 men proceeded on leave. HEBUTERNE church vault reconstructed. Also site of strong point at south end of HEBUTERNE.	

W. Anderson
Capt. R.E.
Cmdg 211th Fd Coy R.E.

2353 Wt. W2514/1454 700,000 5/15 D. D. & L. A.D.S.S./Forms/C. 2118.

Vol 10

CONFIDENTIAL

War Diary
of
211th Field Company R.E.

from Dec 1. '16 to Dec 31. '16

(Volume XII)

Army Form C. 2118.

WAR DIARY
INTELLIGENCE SUMMARY.
(Erase heading not required.)

211th Field Company R.E.

Instructions regarding War Diaries and Intelligence Summaries are contained in F.S. Regs., Part II. and the Staff Manual respectively. Title pages will be prepared in manuscript.

Place	Date	Hour	Summary of Events and Information	Remarks and references to Appendices
COIGNEUX	1.12.16		Work continued on huts at Div. Laundry at ORVILLE, also fixing windows and concreting floor during huts. Putting in floors to huts (at 95% [?] Ambulance), COIGNEUX. Rivetting & trimming "R" type. Repairs to dugout. Leaving and rivetting YANKEE and YOUNG huts and others at 95th F.A. Ambulance. Nissen hut camp on BUS—BAYENCOURT road. Carpenter work at R.A. Camp, making M.T.M. emplacements, latrine seats etc. 3 men proceeded on leave.	
"	2.12.16		Work as on day before. Also putting second inside walls in Officers' Mess at New Camp COUIN. Ablution stand and cookhouse at 92nd Brigade horse lines.	
"	3.12.16		Work as on day before.	
"	4.12.16		Work as on day before.	
"	5.12.16		Work as on day before. Walls of Officers' Mess at New Camp, COUIN, completed. Walls of Sergt's Mess commenced. Repairs to Left Battalion Hd. dugout, HEBUTERNE. New telegraph assembly at ORVILLE. Work on strengthening roof of Soup Kitchen, HEBUTERNE.	
"	6.12.16		Work as on day before. Repairs to pump at AUTHIE.	
"	7.12.16		Work as on day before. One man went on leave.	
"	8.12.16		Work as on day before. 2 men proceeded on leave.	
"	9.12.16		Work on before. Bridge on BUS road repaired. Repairs commenced to well at R.E. Billet, COUIN.	
"	10.12.16		Sections changed round as regards work.	
"	11.12.16		Work as on 9.12.16. Repairs to cellars in the KEEP, HEBUTERNE.	
"	12.12.16		Work as before. Work commenced on laying pipes from COIGNEUX pumping station to ROSSIGNOL FARM. Frame work of hut erected for traffic control post at cross roads on COIGNEUX—SAILLY road. Marking mining cases and lever troughs also continued.	

Army Form C. 2118.

WAR DIARY
INTELLIGENCE SUMMARY. 211th Field Company R.E.

(Erase heading not required.)

Place	Date	Hour	Summary of Events and Information	Remarks and references to Appendices
COIGNEUX	13.12.16		Work as day before. Work commenced on wiring "R" line	
" "	14.12.16		Work as before. 2 men went on leave.	
" "	15.12.16		Work as before. Fixing and glazing windows at 95th Field Ambulance. Control post hut completed. Pumps repaired 170th Bde RFA horse troughs. Making targets and notice boards for Rifle ranges. Fixing shelves in back room at 97th F.A. Ambulance. Putting up arms rack and washing concrete drains. 2 men proceeded on leave.	
" "	16.12.16		Work as before. Pump at trough near WARNIMONT WOOD temporarily repaired	
" "	17.12.16		Work as before. Repairs to entrance of sort Kitchen dugout at HEBUTERNE. Making 3 Kitcher brackets for Ambulance at HEBUTERNE. Wiring round HEBUTERNE commenced	
" "	18.12.16		Work as before. Repairs to boiler at 37 F.A. No. 3 Group. Proposed Div. Baths, AUTHIE, commenced. One man on leave.	
" "	19.12.16		Work as before. Baths at Div. 3 same proposed. Wire commenced on Engine house at pumping Station, COUIN. Also stand for tank at ROSSIGNOL FARM.	
" "	20.12.16		Work as before. Engine house, COUIN, completed.	
" "	21.12.16		Work as before. Repairs to two wells in COUIN. Also pumps near WARNIMONT WOOD repaired. 2 men went on leave.	
" "	22.12.16		Work as before. Work commenced on clearing and rutting YU2. 2 men went on leave.	
" "	23.12.16		Work as before.	
" "	24.12.16		As before. Platform for tank erected at ROSSIGNOL FARM. Repairs commenced to steam engine at ST LEGER. Repairs also commenced to M.G. dugout in R line near WOMAN	

Army Form C. 2118.

WAR DIARY
INTELLIGENCE SUMMARY. 211th Ft. Coy R.E.

(Erase heading not required.)

Place	Date	Hour	Summary of Events and Information	Remarks and references to Appendices
COIGNEUX	25.12.16		Sections changed round. No work done.	
" "	26.12.16		Work as on 24.12.16, except no more work on wiring round HEBUTERNE. Lt. Mullinson went to Div. School, VAUCHELLES, to lecture on Military Engineering.	
"	27.12.16		Work as before. Pipes to ROSSIGNOL FARM tested, and pipes laid to tank near R.9, Dump.	
"	28.12.16		Work as before. Work on M.G. dugouts in YUSSIF and YIDDISH. Putting up wiring traverses in YIDDISH in front of "Q" Line at night. Work commenced on laying 3" pipe line to supply to Div. Train at ST. LEGER. 2 men went on leave.	
"	29.12.16		Work as before. Work commenced on new gumboot store at 157 A BRICK, SAILLY. 2 men went on leave.	
"	30.12.16		Work as before.	
"	31.12.16		Work as before. Repairs to pump near P.O.W. Camp, WARNIMONT WOOD.	

C.W.R. Anderson
Capt. R.E.

Vol XI

CONFIDENTIAL

War Diary

of

211th Field Company R.E.

from 1.1.17 to 31.1.17

(Volume 13).

Army Form C. 2118.

211th Field Company

WAR DIARY
INTELLIGENCE SUMMARY.
(Erase heading not required.)

Place	Date	Hour	Summary of Events and Information	Remarks and references to Appendices
COIGNEUX	1.1.17.		Rest day.	
" "	2.1.17		Work continued on extension of hut at Div. Laundry, ORVILLE. Laying floor at 93rd Field Ambulance, AUTHIE. Building cellar at "B" Farm, HEBUTERNE. Pontoneer work in FANKEE and Q huts near WELCOME. Pumping water out of THORPE. Repairing dugout in R Line south of WOMAN. Laying water pipe to A.S.C. horse lines, ST LEGER. Also pipe line to R.F.A. huts near ROSSIGNOL FARM. Making horse hut by BUS–BAYENCOURT road. Preparing farm work for troops at P.O.W. Camp on BUS–AUTHIE road. Preparing Billet 157A at SAILLY for gun test stay. Building incinerator at AUTHIE. Making revetment frames and painting notice boards.	
" "	3.1.17		Work as on day before. Also work(?) commenced on wiring HEBUTERNE defences. 2 men went on leave. Work begun on revetting YOUNG ST (back baba) and THE NAP.	
" "	4.1.17		Work as on day before. Also erecting 4 canvas blocks on HOWARD. 2 men went on leave.	
" "	5.1.17		No's 1 and 3 Sections left at 8 a.m. by motor lorries, and proceeded to BERNAVILLE and FIENVILLERS, and told are from O/C I/Regn RE. Went on retails to trenches continued. 2 men went on leave. 2 Sections of 217(?) Co. arrived at COIGNEUX.	
" "	6.1.17		Work continued on trenches.	
" "	7.1.17		Work as on day before.	
" "	8.1.17		Packing carts, cleaning up huts, etc. No's 2 and 4 Sections returned from SAILLY-DELL to COIGNEUX.	
" "	9.1.17		Remainder of Company left COIGNEUX at 8 a.m. and proceeded to BERNAVILLE, and billeted there. Stopped midday dry motor lorries for 1 hour. Transport arrived at 7 p.m.	
BERNAVILLE	10.1.17		Reorganised officers, O/C depts (& offices) instruments course for O/Cs Coys at LE PARCQ. 2 men went on leave.	

Army Form C. 2118.

WAR DIARY
or
INTELLIGENCE SUMMARY.

(Erase heading not required.)

2/1 R. Field Coy R.E.

Instructions regarding War Diaries and Intelligence Summaries are contained in F. S. Regs., Part II. and the Staff Manual respectively. Title pages will be prepared in manuscript.

Place	Date	Hour	Summary of Events and Information	Remarks and references to Appendices
BERNAVILLE	11/1/17		Check parade & clean arms inspection. 1/2 Coy finishing frein litter Wk at FIENVILLERS, CANDAS & BERNEUIL. Pre tracking and repairs to fields	
"	12/1/17		2 men went on leave. Wk on tracking continued. Also 3 cook houses started. Party of 30m/keeper. Ote men went on musketry. Wk continuing at FIENVILLERS, CANDAS & BERNEUIL.	
"	13/1/17		LIEUT WOOD and Nos 2 & 6 ORVILLE for wk on Div Laundry. Wk on tracking and cook houses continued. Rifle ranges and drill wk continues at FIENVILLERS, CANDAS & BERNEUIL. Blast at Nr Ammunition & Bomb Depot pushed on rapidly	
"	14/1/17			
"	15/1/17		Remainder of No 2 Section to ORVILLE to join wk continued for wk on tracking &c at AMPLIER. Rifle ranges drill, making roads, tracks, cook houses & &c and wk continued on Cook Houses. Coy finding carting fatigue for bricks from BOIS to Co VAREE at GORGES and taking bricks to Div dump BERNAVILLE. Wk continues at FIENVILLERS, CANDAS.	
"	16/1/17		Rifle drill and musketry continuing. Wk on cook houses (6 off 8 m) and arches & repairs continues. Wire wk starting on bridges and employment of the 6 G.I. transport as day before until trucks, public labour, transport from CANDAS flank to BERNVILLE also fresh prolic carting repair. Wk at FIENVILLERS, CANDAS continued.	
"	17/1/17		Knotting & lashing wk cook and transport as day before.	
"	18/1/17		Rapid training " " 2 men away on leave.	

Army Form C. 2118.

WAR DIARY
or
INTELLIGENCE SUMMARY.   211th Field Coy R.E.

(Erase heading not required.)

Instructions regarding War Diaries and Intelligence Summaries are contained in F.S. Regs., Part II. and the Staff Manual respectively. Title pages will be prepared in manuscript.

Place	Date	Hour	Summary of Events and Information	Remarks and references to Appendices
BERNAVILLE	19/1/17		Rifle exercises &c. Work and transport as day before.	
"	20/1/17		Work continued on huts and latrines at A + Q. C.E. XIII Corps and cookers at stables &c. Our new work in rear. Platoon drill. Work continued as day before. Report is A.60 that one N.C.O. man on leave. Work continued on trenches at BOISBERGUES.	
"	21/1/17		Rifle ammunition took up train. Third & 4th inspection o/c returned from LE PARC Q. Work in trees for green at helly 15.40.	
"	22/1/17		Rifle exercises &c. Work continues. 2/Lt Kinlay + 5 Sappers to OCCOCHES to take over work from 210th Field Coy R.E.	
"	23.1.17		Work as before. Capt. Hoosfoot went on leave.	
"	24.1.17		Work as before. St. Fearile and N.?.4 Section marched from BERNAVILLE to VAUCHELLES for work on Div. School Huts. 2 men went on leave.	
"	25.1.17		Work continued. Work commenced on erecting hutmen huts at Div School and repairing Lectern room.	
"	26.1.17		Work as before. 1 N.C.O. proceeded on leave.	
"	27.1.17		Work as before. Lt. Round and N?.2 Section marched from FIENVILLERS to GEZAINCOURT and billeted there.	
"	28.1.17		Work as before. Lt. Round and N?.2 Section commenced a misens hutment at BAGNEUX. Work continued.	
"	29.1.17		Work continued. W/2 commenced to killer huts. Work commenced on hutmen out from GEZAINCOURT to OCCOCHES to killer them. Huts at OCCOCHES.	

Army Form C. 2118.

WAR DIARY
INTELLIGENCE SUMMARY. 211th Field Company
R.E.

(Erase heading not required.)

Instructions regarding War Diaries and Intelligence Summaries are contained in F. S. Regs., Part II. and the Staff Manual respectively. Title pages will be prepared in manuscript.

Place	Date	Hour	Summary of Events and Information	Remarks and references to Appendices
BERNAVILLE	30.1.17		Work continued. Lt. Round and No. 2 Section and initiated there. Work continued.	
" "	31.1.17		Work commenced and marched from GEZAINCOURT to PERNOIS. Work commenced and hutting and huts & at PERNOIS.	

W. A. Crichton
Major R.E.
Comdg 211th Fd Coy RE

Vol 12

CONFIDENTIAL

War Diary

of

211th Field Company R.E.

from 1.2.17 to 28.2.17

(Volume XIV)

HEADQUARTERS,
31st
DIVISIONAL ENGINEERS.
No. L5641
Date. 2.3.17

WAR DIARY

INTELLIGENCE SUMMARY. 211th Field Company R.E.

Army Form C. 2118.

(Erase heading not required.)

Place	Date	Hour	Summary of Events and Information	Remarks and references to Appendices
BERNAVILLE	1.2.17		Work continued on baths at BOIS BERGUES, making targets, tables and tenders at BERNAVILLE, making cartway road near Div. Laundry at ORVILLE, and putting up tank there. Repairing kitchen room at Div. School, VAUCHELLES. Work on painting at BERNAVILLE.	
"	2.2.17		Work as before. Lt. Mallinson went to Div. School VAUCHELLES. Lecture on military engineering	
"	3.2.17		Work stopped on baths at BOIS BERGUES, and packing & cart commenced. Other work as before.	
"	4.2.17		Packing carts and cleaning up. We shifted. Lt. Farrell proceeded to SAILLY DELL to take over work and billets from 81st Field Coy R.E.	
"	5.2.17		Coy transport left at 8am, and arrived SAILLY DELL 6.30 pm. Rest of Coy left by motor bus at 12 noon. Lt. Farrell went round work on a/c CRE YELLOW LINE with 2 Officers 81st Field Coy R.E. O/c remained at BERNAVILLE.	
SAILLY DELL	6.2.17		Half Coy paraded at 6.45 am for work on our R.E. dumps and levelling & tidying up YELLOW LINE. also finishing same, abeato by Infantry working parties of 19th Division. Other half Coy paraded at 11.30 am for " " " " O/c Capt. Horsford reported Coy from leave. one O.R. returned from leave	
"	7.2.17		a/c Coy reports at office of C.R.E. 19th Division COVIN. Lt. Mallinson reported Coy from Div. School VAUCHELLES. One O.R. rejoined Coy from leave. Work as day before. Lt. Wood & one O.R. on leave.	
"	8.2.17		Work as on day before. one O.R. returns from leave.	
"	9.2.17		Work as on day before.	
"	10.2.17		Work as on day before.	
"	11.2.17		Work as on day before.	
"	12.2.17		Work as on day before.	

Army Form C. 2118.

Instructions regarding War Diaries and Intelligence
Summaries are contained in F. S. Regs., Part II.
and the Staff Manual respectively. Title pages
will be prepared in manuscript.

WAR DIARY
INTELLIGENCE SUMMARY.

211th Field Coy. R.E.

(Erase heading not required.)

Place	Date	Hour	Summary of Events and Information	Remarks and references to Appendices
SAILLY OEU	13.2.17		Work as day before. 1 section withdrawn for wiring YELLOW LINE. 5 p.m. one section paraded for wiring.	
"	14.2.17		Work as day before. Wiring of YELLOW LINE continued.	
"	15.2.17		Work and wiring as day before.	
"	16.2.17		Work and wiring as day before. Lt. R.H. Paddison (S.R.) joined Coy as supernumerary officer. One O.R. returned from leave.	
"	17.2.17		Work as day before.	
"	18.2.17		Work as day before. Wiring of YELLOW LINE continued.	
"	19.2.17		Work and wiring as day before. Instructions received from C.R.E. 19th Division to take over billets and work of 81st & 82nd Field Coys R.E.	
"	20.2.17		Lt. Macgregor took over from 82nd Field Coy R.E. billets & work at BAYENCOURT. 81st " " " " " COIGNEUX. Lt. Paddison	
"	21.2.17		Work as day before. No infantry working parties. Lt. Farrell left Coy to join 5th Field Survey Coy. Coy paraded at 7 a.m. packed carts and marched to BAYENCOURT at 11.30 a.m. Taking over billets of 82nd Field Coy R.E. On reports of arrival to CRE 19th Division and handed over list and description of work of 81st Field Coy RE to 76 210th Field Coy R.E.	
BAYENCOURT	22.2.17		Work continued on YELLOW LINE. Reports to infantry working parties provided by 31st Division.	
"	23.2.17		Work as day before.	
"	24.2.17		Work as day before.	

Army Form C. 2118.

WAR DIARY
INTELLIGENCE SUMMARY.

(Erase heading not required.)

211th Field Coy. R.E.

Instructions regarding War Diaries and Intelligence Summaries are contained in F. S. Regs., Part II. and the Staff Manual respectively. Title pages will be prepared in manuscript.

Place	Date	Hour	Summary of Events and Information	Remarks and references to Appendices
BAYENCOURT	25.2.17		Work as on day report. Lt. Patterson taken to C.C.S. C.R.E. came round camps, workshops, fields. Three lance corporals raised. 2/Lt. Trundl Mirsland & 2/Lt. Smart rejoined Coy from leave.	
" "	26.2.17		Work on rifle range stopped before 9 O.C. on Skag Push. Rifle & wiring practices. Carpenters sent to COIGNEUX at 2 p.m. to mend R.A. truck bridges. Lt West and an N.C.O went out in evening to reconnitre and work out site for C.T. across Ms Maurepas, just south of road which was used by WOMAN to man out after 1st flow of trench. 1 N.C.O. to supervise infantry party (2 Carpenters) lifting. Digging not completed.	
" "	27.2.17		Carpenters working on trench bridges. Repairs commenced to BAYENCOURT baths. Also coupling of pipes from COIGNEUX pumping station to ROSSIGNOL FARM baths. Remainder of Company, Physical drill and football.	
" "	28.2.17		Carpenters commenced work on infantry trench bridges. Repairs to BAYENCOURT baths continued, also work at COIGNEUX pumping station. Work commenced at SAILLY DELL baths.	

Signed
Comdg 211th Fd Coy RE

CONFIDENTIAL.

(ORIGINAL)

WAR DIARY
OF

211TH FIELD COMPANY R.E.

FROM MARCH 1ST 1917   TO   MARCH 31ST 1917

VOLUME 15

Army Form C. 2118.

WAR DIARY
INTELLIGENCE SUMMARY.
(Erase heading not required.)

211th Field Company, R.E.

Place	Date	Hour	Summary of Events and Information	Remarks and references to Appendices
BAYENCOURT	1.3.17		Lt. Mallinson was admitted to Hospital, sick. Company practised rapid wire entanglements. Return to office of Dir. from west of BAILEULMONT mostly hospital Nissen hut on BUS - BAYENCOURT road.	
"	2.3.17		Company did Jacks drill. Work done on nights of various sizes at 95th Field Ambulance, COIGNEUX. Report made from COIGNEUX to bring British ROSSIGNOL FARM. Return to BAYENCOURT Baths.	
"	3.3.17		Company did physical drill. Work done on repairs to pipes at SAILLY DELL water supply.	
"	4.3.17		Company did physical drill. Work examined on making store for 95th Field Ambulance. Also work on ROSSIGNOL FARM Baths.	
"	5.3.17		Work commenced on repairing road from HEBUTERNE via CHURCH and ROSSIGNOL WOOD to BUCQUOY. 2nd Lieut. O.P.S. Fisher joined the Company.	
"	6.3.17		Lt. Round and No.3 Section marked by wooden posts boundary of Lewis School Flew. Work commenced on taking up tram line running through SAILLY DELL. 2nd Lieut. Raddison rejoined the Company from leave.	

Army Form C. 2118.

WAR DIARY
INTELLIGENCE SUMMARY.

215 Field Company R.E.

(Erase heading not required.)

Instructions regarding War Diaries and Intelligence Summaries are contained in F. S. Regs., Part II. and the Staff Manual respectively. Title pages will be prepared in manuscript.

Place	Date	Hour	Summary of Events and Information	Remarks and references to Appendices
BAYENCOURT	7.3.17		C.R.E. gave orders for work from HEBUTERNE to be cleared on a field tramway track. Work done a Nissen hut in grounds of QUIN Chateau. (S in +Q)	
"	8.3.17		Work continued	
"	9.3.17		Work continued	
"	10.3.17		Work continued. Orders received to move to COURCELLES.	
"	11.3.17		Company moved to COURCELLES and billeted there. Work continued as usual.	
COURCELLES	12.3.17		Work commenced a laying tramway from SAILLY to HEBUTERNE. Other work as before. Work on making metal water carriers (pack). Also horse trough at COIGNEUX dump	
"	13.3.17		Work continued. Also repairs to tanks at COURCELLES	
"	14.3.17		Work continued. Tramway completed from SAILLY to HEBUTERNE.	
"	16.3.17		Work continued.	
"	16.3.17		Work continued.	
"	17.3.17		Work continued. Orders as to move received.	
"	18.3.17		Company paraded at 7am for packing up carts and cleaning billets. Parade 9.30 a.m.	

WAR DIARY

INTELLIGENCE SUMMARY. 211th Field Company R.E.

(Erase heading not required.)

Army Form C. 2118.

Instructions regarding War Diaries and Intelligence Summaries are contained in F. S. Regs., Part II and the Staff Manual respectively. Title pages will be prepared in manuscript.

Place	Date	Hour	Summary of Events and Information	Remarks and references to Appendices
			and moved off at 10 a.m., marched to TERRAMESNIL, arriving at 3.30 p.m. and billeted there.	
TERRAMESNIL	19.3.17		Paraded 8 a.m. for cleaning up billets. Paraded 10.30 a.m. marched off 11 a.m. marched to BRETEL, reaching there 12.45 p.m., and billeted there.	
BRETEL	20.3.17		Paraded 9 a.m. for cleaning up billets. Paraded 1.30 p.m. marched off 2 p.m. Reached OCOCHES 3 p.m. Lost waggon did not enter village owing to very wet and soft pavé of road just outside village, left 6 p.m. Billeted there.	
OCOCHES	21.3.17		Cleaned billets 7 a.m. Paraded 8.30 a.m. marched off 9 at 9 a.m. Reached SIBIVILLE at 2.25 p.m. and billeted there. One waggon had to be destroyed, having to its getting bogged.	
SIBIVILLE	22.3.17		Cleaned billets at 7 a.m. Paraded 8.30 a.m. marched off 9 at 9 a.m. Reached 4.OSSART at 1.45 p.m., and billeted them and at BRITEL.	
GROSSART	23.3.17		Company rested here a day. Paraded at 10 a.m. and 2 p.m. for stowing into.	
GROSSART	24.3.17		Paraded 9 a.m. to clear billets. Paraded 8.45 a.m. marched off 9 a.m. Reached FONTAINE LEZ HERMANS at 12.45 p.m., and billeted there.	
FONTAINE-LEZ-HERMANS	25.3.17		Message received 3 a.m. as to change to Summer Time. Paraded 7 a.m. to clear billets. Paraded 8.45 a.m. Marched off 9 a.m. Reached ST VENANT at 12.45 p.m. and billeted there.	

Army Form C. 2118.

WAR DIARY

INTELLIGENCE SUMMARY. 2/1st Field Company R.E.

Instructions regarding War Diaries and Intelligence Summaries are contained in F. S. Regs., Part II and the Staff Manual respectively. Title pages will be prepared in manuscript.

(Erase heading not required.)

Place	Date	Hour	Summary of Events and Information	Remarks and references to Appendices
ST VENANT	26.3.17		Paraded 9am & 2 p.m. for cleaning carts and sharpening tools. No 1 Section 1/2 of Service inoculated. L/Cpl. P. T. CROWTHER R.E. joined for Company. 3 Cleaning & repacking carts and sharpening tools. Nos 2/3 Section inoculated.	
" "	27.3.17			
" "	28.3.17		Preliminary practise with Weldon trestles on land. No. 4 Section inoculated.	
" "	29.3.17		Weldon trestle bridging. Remainder of Company inoculated.	
" "	30.3.17		Pontoon bridging	
" "	31.3.17		Pontoon & trestle bridging	

J. R. Gardner
Major R.E.
Comdg 2/1st Field Coy R.E.

2353 Wt. W2544/7454 700,000 5/15 D. D. & L. A.D.S.S./Forms/C. 2118.

ORIGINAL

CONFIDENTIAL

WAR DIARY

of

THE 247TH FIELD COY. R.E.

FROM APRIL 1ST 1917 TO APRIL 30TH 1917.

VOLUME. XVI.

Army Form C. 2118.

WAR DIARY

INTELLIGENCE SUMMARY: 211th Field Company R.E.

(Erase heading not required.)

Instructions regarding War Diaries and Intelligence Summaries are contained in F.S. Regs., Part II. and the Staff Manual respectively. Title pages will be prepared in manuscript.

Place	Date	Hour	Summary of Events and Information	Remarks and references to Appendices
ST VENANT	1.4.17		Church Parade in morning. Cleaning carts in afternoon.	
" "	2.4.17		Physical drill. Lecture on "Horsemastership". Pontoon and trestle bridging. Musketry exercises and section drill. Lt. Pond proceeded to Div. School VAUCHELLES.	
" "	3.4.17		Pontoon and trestle bridging. Musketry exercises and section drill.	
" "	4.4.17		Lecture on "Strong Points". Digging strong point. Pontoon and trestle bridging.	
" "	5.4.17		Pontoon and trestle bridging. Rapid wiring of strong point.	
" "	6.4.17		Similar trestle bridging.	
" "	7.4.17		Rifling strong point. Similar trestle bridging. Lt. Pond returned to Company.	
" "	8.4.17		Packing carts and cleaning up billets in morning. Paraded at 1 p.m. and marched to GONNEHEM, reaching there at 5 p.m. Billetted there.	
GONNEHEM	9.4.17		Physical drill. Cleaning carts.	
" "	10.4.17		Section drill. Removing mud from roads. 2nd Corpl. Richardson proceeded to ABBEVILLE on receiving a commission.	
" "	11.4.17		Packing carts and cleaning billets in morning. Paraded 12.45 p.m. and marched to MAISNIL-LEZ-RUITZ, reaching there at 5.45 p.m. and billetted there.	
MAISNIL-LEZ-RUITZ	12.4.17		Drill, and scraping mud off the road near billets.	

Army Form C. 2118.

WAR DIARY
INTELLIGENCE SUMMARY. 2/1st Field Company R.E.
(Erase heading not required.)

Instructions regarding War Diaries and Intelligence Summaries are contained in F. S. Regs, Part II and the Staff Manual respectively. Title pages will be prepared in manuscript.

Place	Date	Hour	Summary of Events and Information	Remarks and references to Appendices
MAISNIL-LEZ-RUITZ	13.4.17		Physical drill, section drill, and musketry exercises.	
" "	14.4.17		Paraded 7 a.m. for cleaning up billets. Paraded at 8 a.m and marched to GUESTREVILLE reaching there at 12 noon. Billetted there.	
GUESTREVILLE	15.4.17		Cleaning roads near billets. Drill in afternoon.	
" "	16.4.17		Drill in morning. Football in afternoon.	
" "	17.4.17		Cleaning up billets and packing carts. Paraded at 2 p.m and marched to ECOIVRES. Billeting Men in X Huts.	
ECOIVRES	18.4.17		Taking down Nissen huts in X Hutments, for transfer further forward.	
" "	19.4.17		3 sections taking down Nissen huts. One section working on repairs and drainage of ECOIVRES - MONT ST ELOY road with a company from 188th Inf. Bde.	
" "	20.4.17		One section taking down Nissen huts. One section on road as before. One section repairing roads in billets in ECOIVRES. One section commenced work on shelters to food dumps at HAUTE-AVESNES. Orders to move received.	
" "	21.4.17		Cleaning up billets and packing carts. Paraded at 11.15 a.m and marched behind the 1st D.L.I. to ST NICHOLAS. It. Wood and No.2 Section left billets at ECOIVRES to complete food dump shelters. Company went on to	

Army Form C. 2118.

WAR DIARY
INTELLIGENCE SUMMARY.
(Erase heading not required.)

211th Field Company R.E.

Instructions regarding War Diaries and Intelligence Summaries are contained in F.S. Regs., Part II. and the Staff Manual respectively. Title pages will be prepared in manuscript.

Place	Date	Hour	Summary of Events and Information	Remarks and references to Appendices
ST NICHOLAS	21.4.17 (cont'd)		Camp try ST NICHOLAS - ROCLINCOURT road, near LES 4 VENTS.	
	22.4.17		Commenced work with 18th D.L.I. on light railway track from ST NICHOLAS towards BAILLEUL.	
"	23.4.17		Work continued on light railway track.	
"	24.4.17		A/Capt Murray left Company to join a Rly. Construction Depot. Work on railway continued. Captain F. Hardport and Lt R.H Paddison were both wounded, and admitted to hospital. Neither seriously. Lt Wood and N.º 2 Section rejoined Company	
"	25.4.17		Work continued on clearing railway track.	
"	26.4.17		Work as before.	
"	27.4.17		Work as before. Lt 1st Cpl and a Sapper wounded.	
"	28.4.17		Commenced laying track. 18th D.L.I. left off work at 12 noon, having had orders to man off as soon as possible as reserve to 63rd R.N. Division.	
"	29.4.17		Continued laying track.	
"	30.4.17		Nos 1 + 2 sects Q? stacking Iny and cleaning captured war material, nos 3 +4 Sections continued laying track.	

Lt Pound
LATE
OC 211 Fd Coy RE

ORIGINAL

Vol 15

CONFIDENTIAL

WAR DIARY
OF

From May 1st 1917 To May 31st 1917

VOLUME XVII

WAR DIARY 211 Field Coy R.E.
INTELLIGENCE SUMMARY for May 1917.

Army Form C. 2118.

(Erase heading not required.)

Place	Date	Hour	Summary of Events and Information	Remarks and references to Appendices
	MAY 1		Nos. 1 & 2 Sections start fly and cleaners continued war material.	
			Nos. 3 & 4 marched to dugout in Railway cutting S.W. of BAILLEUL.	
	1/2	Night	Nos. 1 & 5 WOOD & CROWTHER Subways highly twenty trenches.	
	2	Day	Nos. 3 & 4 Sections cleaning dugouts ready to move in.	
			marched to near WEST of BAILLEUL	
	3/4	Night	Day Staff went on 12th Bn R. Scot Division and gave first firing troop with start finish on 12th flank of the Division. Using line here Trench M1180 etc - M320 etc.	
	4/5		Parties ayild work continued	
	5/6		Attempted R continued work but prevented by heavy enemy Barrage and expected attack handed out trench. Took up fifth hop south of OPPY contour	
	6/7	day	No 1 & No 2 & No 5 flats going to CROWTHER M16 & then erected Riley's Gaps & Sections MID Breastworks between hedge & front M28 to OPPY.	
		night	When in added Zeil. Thorne close dugn mortared severely wounded	
	7	day	Remained in second position abandoned by 2/6 by Workers No 3 & 5 sections fly wire cleaning end due to 2nd Bomb.	
	8			
	9		Work continued. Also erecting cookhouse + latrines wires for A.F.M.	

WAR DIARY
or
INTELLIGENCE SUMMARY.
(Erase heading not required.)

Army Form C. 2118.

Place	Date	Hour	Summary of Events and Information	Remarks and references to Appendices
	May 10		Work as previous day.	
	11		(i) Lt. A. BLAIR reported for duty.	
	12		(ii) Lts. WINFIELD & BLAIR reconnoitred lines & inspected C.T.s & REDLINE.	
	15		MAJOR R.A.S. MARSEL took over command of the Company from MAJOR GUIDO.	
	21/22	night	Started work on RED LINE. Junior Subalterns detailed to put Infantry who are doing the work. In Corps how a similar No to their section being left after each section. The sections now are 5 in number & drawn NO 1, NO 2, NO 3, NO 4, NO 5. No 5. We opening started about 10 pm and at 4 hours. One Officer and about 6 Subs to 20 Infantrymen, and sections to the work sent to next camp. R. Lt. BLAIR detailed always to the work.	
	22			
	26/27 27/28	night night	(iii) Lts. PRINGLE S.C. BUTON & E. ENTER arrived Sapper S. ENTON admitted Hosp.	
	29		Sgt. REEVE went on leave. Spare horse issued to Company. Two men issued to M.G. base to RED LINE.	
	30		(iii) Lt. F. KEATING reported for duty.	

ORIGINAL

CONFIDENTIAL

WAR DIARY

OF

211TH FIELD COMPANY R.E.

From June 1st 1917 To June 30th 1917

(Volume XVIII)

Army Form C. 2118.

WAR DIARY 211 Fd Coy RE
or
INTELLIGENCE SUMMARY for June 1917

(Erase heading not required.)

Place	Date	Hour	Summary of Events and Information	Remarks and references to Appendices
4 Vents in ARRAS.	June 1		8 Remounts arrived. Coy working on RED LINE on whole of Corps front.	
"	2		16 Reinforcements arrived. 59th Field Coy of 5th Division took over work on the RED LINE on the Northern half of the Corps front. Sgt. BONNER went on one months leave.	
"	3		93rd Infantry Bde relieved 92nd Infantry Bde on RED LINE on Southern half of Corps front.	
"	4		No. 2 Section relieved No 3 and No 1 relieved No 4 on RED LINE	
"	5		Capt. HORSPOOL rejoined Company on recovery from wounds	
"	6/7	Night	No work done on RED LINE	
"	7/8		On Right Sector of RED LINE 18th WEST YORKS Regt. and No 3 Section relieved No 2. On Left Sector 15th WEST YORKS Regt relieved 18th WEST YORKS Regt. and No 4 Section relieved No 1. 11 LtR&AR relieved 16th West Yorks Regt. and No 4 Section relieved No 1. 11 LtR&AR with a working party of 180 provided by the 93rd Infantry Bde and a few Sappers started work on the RED LINE	
"	8/9		Sapper BENNETT wounded.	
"	9/10		No work done on RED LINE.	

WAR DIARY 211th Coy. R.E.
INTELLIGENCE SUMMARY.
for June 1917. continued

Army Form C. 2118.

Place	Date	Hour	Summary of Events and Information	Remarks and references to Appendices
4 Vents near ARRAS.	June 10		Company relieved the 248th Field Coy of the 63rd R.N. Division in work in rear area of the LEFT Bde in the front line. Handed work on RED LINE over to 249th Field Coy of the 63rd R.N. Division. 94th Infantry Bde Instr over L/F Bde area extending from OPPY to GAVRELLE. Nos. 1+2 sections marched to quarters in trench just behind the crest of the ridge WEST of BAILLEUL.	
	19/11	Night	Nos 1+2 sections started work supervising Infantry working parties digging communication and support trenches.	
	12	Day	Finished work on G.O.C's Dugouts	
	13/14	Night	2nd Infantry Bde started providing working parties in LEFT Bde area.	
	14/15	"	Nos. 1+2 sections did rest work.	
	15	Day	No 3 section relieved No 2 and No 4 relieved No 1	
	18	"	Divisional Horse Show held.	
	19/20	Night	92nd Infantry Bde relieved 94th Infantry Bde in L/F Bde area. Lt. BLAIR returned to camp at	
	20	Day	No 1 section relieved No 4 & No 2 relieved No 3. 4 Vents.	

Army Form C. 2118.

WAR DIARY 211 Fd. Coy. R.E.
INTELLIGENCE SUMMARY.
for June 1917 contined

(Erase heading not required.)

Place	Date	Hour	Summary of Events and Information	Remarks and references to Appendices
	June			
4 Vents	22		Capt. POUND joined forward sections.	
near ARRAS	23		MAJOR MANSEL returned to 4 Vents.	
	25		No 4 section relieved No 1 and No 3 relieved No 2.	
	26/27	Night	94th Infantry Bde relieved 93rd Infantry Bde.	
	27	Day	Preparations for attack completed.	
	28	"	Attack by 94th Infantry Bde at 7.10 p.m. CAPT HURSPOOL relieved WEST POUND.	
	29/30	Night	Nos 3 + 4 sections setting down telegraph poles in ground captured the day before

CONFIDENTIAL

WAR DIARY OF THE

211TH FIELD COMPANY R.E.

FROM 1st JULY 1917 TO 31st JULY 1917

(VOLUME XIX)

ORIGINAL

Army Form C. 2118.

WAR DIARY of 2/1st Field Coy. R.E.

INTELLIGENCE SUMMARY.
(Erase heading not required.)

Instructions regarding War Diaries and Intelligence Summaries are contained in F.S. Regs., Part II. and the Staff Manual respectively. Title pages will be prepared in manuscript.

Place	Date	Hour	Summary of Events and Information	Remarks and references to Appendices
ST NICHOLAS	1/7/17		2 Forward Sections clearing VISCOUNT STREET C.T. 2 Rear Sections painting and repairing transport. Sharpening tools and completing Officers' Quarters.	
"	2/7/17		Work as day before. 6 O.R. went on leave.	
"	3/7/17		Forward work and wiring to trenches over No. 1 Area at 240th Field Coy R.E. 2 forward sections respectively in reserve roof of Coy at 4 sections.	
"	4/7/17		Rest of Coy preparing for move. Coy photos at 8 a.m. and march to A.C.Q. Tidying up billets.	
A.C.Q	5/7/17		Coy on work of trucking. Improving billets, drainage room making, latrines to camp. O/C took over duties of A/C.R.E.	
"	6/7/17		5 O.R. went on leave. Work as day before.	
"	7/7/17		" "	
"	8/7/17		attached for work to C.R.E. XIII Corps. Lt. Pound & 5 O.R. went on leave. 11 Lt. Fisher evacuated.	
"	9/7/17		Company training. 11 Lt. Blair to Hospital. 4 O.R. rejoined Coy from Base.	
"	10/7/17		" 4 Sections through gas chamber.	
"	11/7/17		" "	
"	12/7/17		Company preparing for move. N°4 Section dismantling Bowel huts. 6 O.R. went on leave. Capt Hospital, Lt. Lapin & 4 Section Sergt took out work please from 1st Canadian Field Coy. Lt Winfield took over work of plans from 107th Canadian Pioneer Sup Battn.	
"	13/7/17		Company less N°4 Section travel at 1 a.m. and march to AUX RIETZ Railway Sidings at 3.15 a.m. 2 sections move into forward billets at PETIT VIMY. N°4 Section continued work of dismantling Bowel huts.	

Army Form C. 2118.

Instructions regarding War Diaries and Intelligence Summaries are contained in F. S. Regs., Part II. and the Staff Manual respectively. Title pages will be prepared in manuscript.

WAR DIARY of 211th (Field) Coy R.E.

INTELLIGENCE SUMMARY.

(Erase heading not required.)

Place	Date	Hour	Summary of Events and Information	Remarks and references to Appendices
AUX RIETZ	14/7/17		2 Forward Section employed on work of clearing and broadening C.T.'s and new new front line." Reft section on trunking field, near new horse lines. Balance of 10 O.R. went on leave. No.4 section no day before.	
"	15/7/17		Work as day before. No.4 Section reforming Coy.	
"	16/7/17		Work as day before. 2 Rear section as day before on trucking horselines Platoon &c	
"	17/7/17		Work as day before 10 O.R. went on leave.	
"	18/7/17		Work as day before with the addition for the 2 forward sections of work on new C.T. O/c rejoins Coy.	
"	19/7/17		Work as day before with the exception of work in connection with new front line.	
"	20/7/17		Work as day before. Rear sections changed over. Pl. Pound rejoins Coy. 11 O.R. went on leave.	
"	21/7/17		Work as day before, with the exception of work on new C.T. and the addition of reforming tramway.	
"	22/7/17		Work as day before. 2 Rear Sections dismantling & removing 2 Mission huts also.	
"	23/7/17		Work as day before with the exception of preparing to tramway, and the addition of work on new C.T. and Platoon at Pompoire and Capt Hereford. 9 O.R. went on leave.	
"	24/7/17		Work as day before.	
"	25/7/17		Work as day before with the exception of work on new C.T.	
"	26/7/17		Work as day before with the addition of work on sheet trench &c. 11 O.R. went on leave.	
"	27/7/17		Work as day before.	
"	28/7/17		Work as day before.	
"	29/7/17		Forward & Rear sections changed over. Work done by forward section on clearing & wire trenching C.T.'s only. Work of rear section no before.	

11 O.R. went on leave.

2353 Wt. W2544/1454 700,000 5/15 D. D. & L. A.D.S.S./Forms/C. 2118.

Army Form C. 2118.

WAR DIARY of 211th Field Coy R.E.

INTELLIGENCE SUMMARY.

(Erase heading not required.)

Instructions regarding War Diaries and Intelligence Summaries are contained in F. S. Regs., Part II and the Staff Manual respectively. Title pages will be prepared in manuscript.

Place	Date	Hour	Summary of Events and Information	Remarks and references to Appendices
AUX RIETZ	30/7/17		Work as day before.	
"	31/7/17		Work as day before.	

J. Horsford Capt. R.E.
for O/c 211th Field Coy R.E.

CONFIDENTIAL

WAR DIARY
(ORIGINAL)
OF

211TH FIELD COMPANY R.E.

From 1st August 1917 To 31st August 1917

VOLUME XX

Army Form C. 2118.

WAR DIARY of 211th Field Coy R.E.

INTELLIGENCE SUMMARY.

(Erase heading not required.)

Instructions regarding War Diaries and Intelligence Summaries are contained in F. S. Regs., Part II. and the Staff Manual respectively. Title pages will be prepared in manuscript.

Place	Date	Hour	Summary of Events and Information	Remarks and references to Appendices
AUX RIETZ	1/8/17		2 Sections on work of building Horsestandings and dugouts. 1 section on dummy railway which Sandbags and concrete dugouts forward area	
"	2/8/17		2 Sections on work as following & 1 O.R. & 10 O.R. to hospital	
"	3/8/17		Work as day before	
"	4/8/17		Work as day before	
"	5/8/17		Work as day before. Capt F. HOUSDEN returned from leave	
"	6/8/17		Work as day before. 5 O.R. went on leave	
"	7/8/17		Work as day before. 2 2nd Lieuts RULE and J HOLE returned from leave	
"	8/8/17		Work as day before. 2/Lt J E WINFIELD & 1 O.R. went on leave	
"	9/8/17		Work as day before. 1 O.R. to hospital & 2 O.R. admitted to hospital 2nd Lieut LAWN to school	
"	10/8/17		Work as day before. 5 O.R. went on leave	
"	11/8/17		Work as day before	
"	12/8/17		Work as day before	
"	13/8/17		Work as day before. 5 O.R. went on leave	
"	14/8/17		Work as day before	
"	15/8/17		Work as day before. 2 2nd Lieuts and 2 O.R. went on leave	
"	16/8/17		Work as day before. 5 O.R. went on leave	

WAR DIARY of 2/1st Field Coy. RE (South)

Army Form C. 2118.

INTELLIGENCE SUMMARY.
(Erase heading not required.)

Instructions regarding War Diaries and Intelligence Summaries are contained in F. S. Regs., Part II and the Staff Manual respectively. Title pages will be prepared in manuscript.

Place	Date	Hour	Summary of Events and Information	Remarks and references to Appendices
AUX RIETZ	17/8/17		Work as day before. Lt C.P. WOOD returned from leave.	
"	18/8/17		Work as day before. O/C went on leave.	
"	19/8/17		Work as day before.	
"	20/8/17		Work as day before. 2nd Lt J.E. WINFIELD returned from leave.	
"	21/8/17		Work as day before.	
"	22/8/17		Work as day before.	
"	23/8/17		Work as day before.	
"	24/8/17		Work as day before. 2nd Lieut COLE and 2nd Lieut one section changed over.	
"	25/8/17		Work as day before.	
"	26/8/17		Work as day before.	
"	27/8/17		Work as day before.	
"	28/8/17		Work as day before. 1 O.R. went on leave.	
"	29/8/17		Work as day before. N.S.4193 Cpl ond BERETT (Supply Company)	
"	30/8/17		Work as day before. O/C returned from leave.	
"	31/8/17		Work as day before.	

F Hughs Capre
O/C

ORIGINAL

Vol 19

CONFIDENTIAL

WAR DIARY

OF

THE 211TH FIELD COY RE

FROM 1ST SEPT 1917 TO 30TH SEPT 1917

(VOLUME XXI)

Army Form C. 2118.

Instructions regarding War Diaries and Intelligence
Summaries are contained in F.S. Regs., Part II.
and the Staff Manual respectively. Title pages
will be prepared in manuscript.

WAR DIARY
or
INTELLIGENCE SUMMARY.
(Erase heading not required.)

Place	Date	Hour	Summary of Events and Information	Remarks and references to Appendices
Aux Rietz	Sept 17 1st		Major Manuel to Commanding Officers Conference at Bulogne. — Collecting materials and ammunition for Divisional Headquarters at Bois-Carré. (A.26.b.4.7) and C.R.E.'s camp. Also materials for railway. Two bridge (foot and transport) commenced. Erecting water standings at Aux Rietz camp. Nos 3 and 4 Sections working forward billets in cellars and dug-outs in and about Petit Vimy, with amounts of :— building English shelters (three) for Battalion Headquarters in Trench Fort Quary and protecting with sandbags, duckboarding from the Canada German Luslin, New Brunswick and Saxowoo home trenches. Revetting Piggy trench where passing through the railway by Vimy station, forming sump complete with pumps and stretcher rests in Piggy Trench, fitting gas curtains to dug-outs in the neighbourhood. Began erecting Divisional H.Q. huts and farming roads. — Began erecting Nissen hut for men new camp at Ecurie. (A.21.a.7.5)	
	3rd		Nos 3 and 4 Sections in accordance with high explosive bombardment at Petit Vimy, many men wounded. The gas was sent over with the men were staying from about 12.10 a.m. till 2 a.m.	
	5th			
	6th		Nos 3 and 4 return from Petit Vimy to camp at Aux Rietz. Two men sent to hospital from its effects of gas bombardment. — Erecting Nissen huts at White House, Mt. St. Eloi. Commenced erecting Nissen hut camp for Divisional Musketry School at Tornay. —	

WAR DIARY
or
INTELLIGENCE SUMMARY.
(Erase heading not required.)

Army Form C. 2118.

Instructions regarding War Diaries and Intelligence Summaries are contained in F. S. Regs., Part II and the Staff Manual respectively. Title pages will be prepared in manuscript.

Place	Date	Hour	Summary of Events and Information	Remarks and references to Appendices
	6th (continued)		Erecting Nissen Huts for Divisional Train (A.D.S.9) — Offd Letter, permit to run new camp at Ecurie to erect Nissen huts.	
	7th		Finished dismantling Divisional Cinema.	
	8th		Lieut Pound attached to Divisional Artillery — Another movement at 8pm Blitz to 2nd Canadian Field Coy, Canadian Engineers — Bivouacked 3 a.m. and marched to new camp at Ecurie (A.29.a.7.5)	
Ecurie.	9th		Major Murrell returns from Boulogne. — Levelling site Boehmer — (sixty unused) — work & laying floor, finishing roof and making and fitting racks for men. Bray rifle range, altering and reconstructing target board. Boundary and infantry revolving targets — bullet and bayonet trench Army, erecting backward and upward and fitting up apparatus for disappearing targets. — Chiefs Reels mounted registering from enemy aeroplane while working on R.E. park at Belencourt. — Lieut Hopkins accounts injured.	
	10th			
	11th		Repairing and experimenting with Bangalore torpedo to use Lamp. — Twenty Officers Hut camp for Divisional gas officer. — Dismantling Divisional Kinder? Photo? hut at Montagueres and preparing materials for removal to A.29.c.7.6. — also 3 Lorries	

Army Form C. 2118.

WAR DIARY
or
INTELLIGENCE SUMMARY.
(Erase heading not required.)

Place	Date	Hour	Summary of Events and Information	Remarks and references to Appendices
	12th		(continued) move with forward R.H.Q at Carlin for work with Divisional Artillery under Lieut Rand 2nd Lieut Burfield employed here.	
	13th		Commenced erecting Divisional Headquarters at A.29.c.7.6. also O.R.E camps and huts and camps for signals R.F.A, Heavy Artillery, Royal Field Artillery, Gas officer, forming road to D.H.Q., dusk boarding camp. — etc. 3 section commenced work for Artillery consisting of covered and steel gun pits at Willerval, supervising R.F.A. a carrying, dug outs frying gas curtains to dug outs, shooting cellars. — Three O.Rs attached to infantry to teach swing for three days.	
	14th		Making furniture for C.R.A and forming partitions in hut. — Four infantry officers under a course of instruction for Junior officers.	
	15th		Mow gun post site, Roclincourt, work of erection commenced.	
	16th		Erecting Nissen huts at Cape Ammunition filling point.	
	17th		2nd Lieut Winfield and I.O.R. to Mouchecourt in Camouflage course.	
	19th		Erecting Nissen standings for 170th Bgn. R.F.A.	
	21st		Erecting Nissen huts for 93rd Field Ambulance at Roclincourt. — Putting Sugar Bar in a state of defence; work commenced. — 2d Lieut Winfield and I.O.R. returned from Mouchecourt.	
	22nd		2nd Lieut Burfield returned from leave.	

Army Form C. 2118.

WAR DIARY
or
INTELLIGENCE SUMMARY.
(Erase heading not required.)

Place	Date	Hour	Summary of Events and Information	Remarks and references to Appendices
	25th		Driver Carey accidentally injured. — Excavating for rifle range on Vineyard Camp at A, 22, C, 4, 0. work commenced.	
	26th		Driver Bradshaw W. accidentally injured. — Began systematically destroying all unexploded shells, bombs, grenades and other articles of an explosive nature.	
	27th		Sapper Edwards accidentally injured.	
	29th		Capt. Armfort and 1.O.R. to course at First Army Cadet Establet. — Junior officers finished course and were taken over by the 210th and 223rd Field bys. for two days instruction in the line. — Driver Bell accidentally injured.	

Original

Vol 20

CONFIDENTIAL

WAR DIARY

OF

THE 211TH FIELD COY R.E.

FROM 1ST OCT 1917 TO 31ST OCT 1917.

VOLUME XII

WAR DIARY or INTELLIGENCE SUMMARY.

Army Form C. 2118.

Place	Date	Hour	Summary of Events and Information	Remarks and references to Appendices
ECURIE A.27.a.7.6	1917 Oct 1		Work continued from last month: Erecting DIV. H.Q. A.27.c.7.6.; Constructing SPRING LAKE CAMP Rifle Range, A.23.c.4.0.; BRAY Rifle Range and Bayonet Course, F.20.c.7.5.; SUGAR POST Strong Point, B.16.a.x.6.; Erecting Gun Boat Store, ACHICOURT (for Div.Arty.) A.29.c.9.1.; 93rd Field Amb. Billets A.27.c.7.4.; 211th Field Co. R.E. Billets and Horse Standings A.27.a.7.5.; Destroying Mud Shells in Divisional Area, Repairing erection of Mules Horse Standings, all Divisional Units, Constructing Gun emplacements, dug-outs, etc. for 165th and 170th Brigades R.F.A.	Progress refs. FRANCE 57.B.N.W.
	" 2	Coy. S.M. 10 HRS	slightly injured by shell fire. Work continued as above.	
	" 3	"	"	
	" 5	"	; starts erection Church Army Hut A.29.c.5.4.	
	" 6	"	; started repairs ACHICOURT West Camp A.23.c.6.8.	
	" 7	"	Summer time ended at 1 A.M. ;	
	" 8	"	Compelled BRAY Rifle Range & F.20.c.7.5., Guild of Bishops to Rick.	
	" 9	"	2/Lt. FISHER reported from 134 Coys.	Th.30 Killed
	" 10	"	; Started repairs in Billets MT. ST ELOI at TOWNS.	
	" 11/12	"	"	
	" 13	"	; Started repairs in Wells, FARBUS	

WAR DIARY
or
INTELLIGENCE SUMMARY.
(Erase heading not required.)

Army Form C. 2118.

Place	Date	Hour	Summary of Events and Information	Remarks and references to Appendices
	1917 Oct 14		Work continued as preceding; Pioneer Officer's Course started; 93rd Field Amb. Billets Completed	
	" 15		" " ; Completed SPRINGFIELD Camp Rifle Range. A22 c 4.0.	
	" 16/20		" "	
	" 21		2/Lt ADLAIR went on leave.	
	" 22		Started work at SALVAGE DUMP. A27 & 7.7.	
	" 23		Completed Repairs to Wells, FARBUS; Started Road Repairs BAILEYWOOD – ECURIE B.10.B	
	" 24/28		27th Pioneer Officers Course finished.	
	" 29		Completed SPRINGFIELD Camp Rifle Range and Motor Cycle Track THREED HILLS	
	" 30		Started Horse Mange Dip at ECURIE RAILHEAD.	
	" 31		Work still under construction: Erecting Div. H.Q.; Constructing SUGAR POST Strong Point; Erecting Gun Post & Dugout Store at ROEUXCOURT; 211 Field Coy Winter Quarters; Supervising erection of Nissen Huts – Starting for Divisional Units; Construction of Gun emplacements for Siri Artillery; Repairs to Church Army Hut; Repairs to ROEUXCOURT WEST Camp; Repairs to Billets Mt ST. ELOI & ECURIES; Road Repairs BRAY JUNC. – Horse Mange Dip at ECURIE RAILHEAD; Construction at SALVAGE DUMP.	
	" 31		Sapper E. HARROP killed by shell fire.	

Alexander Main. 2/Lt E.
pn of / COMMANDING
211TH FIELD COMPANY R.E.

CONFIDENTIAL

WAR DIARY
OF
THE 211TH FIELD COY. R.E.

From 1-11-17 To 30-11-17

VOLUME XXIII

ORIGINAL

Army Form C. 2118.

WAR DIARY of 211th Field Coy. R.E.

INTELLIGENCE SUMMARY.

(Erase heading not required.)

Instructions regarding War Diaries and Intelligence Summaries are contained in F. S. Regs., Part II and the Staff Manual respectively. Title pages will be prepared in manuscript.

Place	Date	Hour	Summary of Events and Information	Remarks and references to Appendices
ECURIE	1/11/17		No. 3 Section on work in forward area for R.A. No.s 1 & 4 Sections on Gunpits at No. work on Corps Camps ROCLINCOURT (West) Camp repairing NISSEN HUTS. in tank area. No. 2 with the C.R.E. CORPS Troops at ECHOIVRES and GUM BOAT dump Room. Valerye dump. Repairing narrow ge. 3ft 6 in. at No. 2 Section on work at SUGAR POST in forward area.	
"	2/11/17		Work as no day type.	
"	3/11/17		" " " "	Sunday.
"	4/11/17		14 O.R. of No. 2 Section reported Coy from ECROIVRES. No. 3 Section work as no day type. CAPT HORSPOOL reported Coy from 1 Wembley School of Instruction.	
"	5/11/17		No. 2 Section on work in forward area for R.A. No.s 1 & 4 Sections on Gunpits 3ft 6in work on Corps Camps ROCLINCOURT (West) Camps repairing NISSEN HUTS in tank area. No. 2 on work for E.R.E. CORPS Trps at ECHOIVRES and GUM BOAT drying Room + Valerye dump drying Room + 4 O.R. of No. 2 Section on work at SUGAR POST in forward area.	
"	6/11/17		Work as no day type.	
"	7/11/17		Work as no day type.	
"	8/11/17		Work as no day type. 1 O.R. went on leave.	
"	9/11/17		Work as no day type. Took the addresses of members of DIVN Canteen at ROCLINCOURT.	
"	10/11/17		Work as no day type.	
"	11/11/17		No. 3 Section work as no day type.	Sunday.
"	12/11/17		No. 3 Section on work in forward area for R.A. No.s 1 & 4 Section on Gunpits 3ft 6in work on Corps Camp ROCLINCOURT (West) Camp repairing NISSEN HUTS in tank area. No. 2 on work for C.R.E. CORPS Trps at ECHOIVRES and GUM BOAT drying Room + Valerye dump drying Room + 4 O.R. of No. 2 Section on work at SUGAR POST in forward area.	

WAR DIARY of 211th Field Coy R.E. (cont)

INTELLIGENCE SUMMARY.

Army Form C. 2118.

(Erase heading not required.)

Place	Date	Hour	Summary of Events and Information	Remarks and references to Appendices
ECURIE	13/11/17		Work as on day before. LT. D. CALDECOTT went on leave.	
"	14/11/17		Work as on day before until the addition of work on FOURIE WOOD Camp & repair NISSEN HUTS.	
"	15/11/17		Work as on day before.	
"	16/11/17		Work as on day before.	
"	17/11/17		Work as on day before. No 3 Section reported for work from forward area. CAPT. GT. POUND & 1 O.R. report to adjoint Army Bridge Section at ARE. N.C.O. and 3 O.R. on work for C.R.E. CORPS of Guard. CAPT JOSEPH. O.C. Co. works in forward area from 578th Field Coy R.E. again today.	
"	18/11/17		No 1 Section moved to forward area. Likely grey work up. R.A. LOWOOD H. LT. R.E. FISHER × 8 LT J.E. WINFIELD and No 2 + 4 Section moved from HULM (-) unit of 518th field Coy R.E. Works Commanded by Major B.B. Wedge (west) Camp and Shelly room at valance dump from Forres (-) work as on day before.	
"	20/11/17			
"	21/11/17		Work as on day before. CAPT W.M. SKILLINGS again our-Superintend Coy. (Adjacent R.E.) attached to the Coy. Work as on day before.	
"	22/11/17			
"	23/11/17		Work as on day before. 1 OR went on leave.	
"	24/11/17		Work as on day before. 2 OR went on leave.	
"	25/11/17		M.G. Corps hurts only work as day before	
"	26/11/17		No 1 & No 4 Section work as day before. No 3 Section continues work in forward area N. I.N.C. and 3 O.R. opening up from depot for C.R.E. Co for purpose. Work as day before until the addition of work on ECURIE wash Camp + tank area. repair NISSEN HUTS. 2 OR went on leave for annual reinforcements	

Army Form C. 2118.

WAR DIARY of 211th Field Coy R.E. (Army)

INTELLIGENCE SUMMARY.

(Erase heading not required.)

Instructions regarding War Diaries and Intelligence Summaries are contained in F. S. Regs., Part II and the Staff Manual respectively. Title pages will be prepared in manuscript.

Place	Date	Hour	Summary of Events and Information	Remarks and references to Appendices
ECURIE	28/11/17		Works as in day before. Lt D. CALDECOTT returned from leave.	
"	29/11/17		Works as on day before. 1 O.R. wounded.	
"	30/11/17		Works as on day before with the addition of work on HORSE DIP at ECURIE. RAILHEAD taken over from 21st Divn.	

Herbert Capt RE
OC 211th Army Coy RE

Confidential

Volume XXIV

War Diary.

211th Field Company R.E.   31st Division

December 1917.

Army Form C. 2118.

WAR DIARY of 211th Field Coy R.E.
of
INTELLIGENCE SUMMARY.
(Erase heading not required.)

Instructions regarding War Diaries and Intelligence Summaries are contained in F. S. Regs., Part II and the Staff Manual respectively. Title pages will be prepared in manuscript.

Place	Date	Hour	Summary of Events and Information	Remarks and references to Appendices
ECURIE	1917 December 3rd		Captain G. T. Doudd R.E. and Sergeant Mawson J. returned from heavy bridging work at AIRE. No 2 and 4 Sections working in FORWARD AREA. No 2 Section laying trench board and widening BELVOIR TRENCH and TONY TRENCH, forming WATER POINT near FRONT LINE. No 4 Section building camps at CHANTICLEER (ROUNDAY CAMP) and erecting GUM BOOT STORE in BAILLEUL - FAMPOUX ROAD, SOUTH of GAVRELLE - ARRAS ROAD. Cleaning out and filling in shell holes on BAILLEUL AKRAS ROAD.	
			No 3 Section working in BACK AREA. Repairing nissen huts at No 6 Camp. ROCLINCOURT WEST and at ECURIE WOOD CAMP. Constructing horse slipping tent at ECURIE RAILHEAD. No 1 Section working FORWARD assisting Artillery constructing GUN-PITS, DUG-OUTS, OBSERVATION POSTS ETC.	
	4th		11 Lieut A. Blair R.E. attached to 310th Field Coy R.E.	
	7th		The Company paraded at 9-50 A.M. to march out of ECURIE and moved off at 10-15 A.M. March to MARDEUIL arriving at 12 noon. Horses and camp and work to 413th Field Coy R.E. 55th Div.	
MARDEUIL	8th		Commenced training at MARDEUIL	
"	11th		Lieut C.P. Wood M.C. R.E. left company for England for transfer to TANK CORPS	
"	12th		11 Lieut R.E.S. Fisher R.E. attached to 810th Field Coy R.E. 11 Lieut J.E. Winfield R.E. instructing Artillery in wiring	

Army Form C. 2118.

WAR DIARY of 211th Field Coy R.E.
INTELLIGENCE SUMMARY.
(Erase heading not required.)

Instructions regarding War Diaries and Intelligence Summaries are contained in F.S. Regs., Part II. and the Staff Manual respectively. Title pages will be prepared in manuscript.

Place	Date	Hour	Summary of Events and Information	Remarks and references to Appendices
MARoeuil	1917 December 14th		2" Lieut H.W. Bush R.E. joined the company from Base for duty.	
"	15th		Captain F. Horspool R.E. went on leave to England.	
"	20th		No.s 1 and 3 Sections moved out of Maroeuil to forward billets on Vancouver Road.	
"	21st		Remainder of company paraded at 1 P.M. to march out of Maroeuil. Arrived at camp previously vacated at Ecurie taking over from the 413th Field Coy. R.E. 53rd Division.	
ECURIE	"		2" Lieut. R.E.S. Fisher R.E. rejoined company from the 213th Field Coy. R.E.	
"	22nd		2" Lieut. R.E.S. Fisher R.E. went to forward billets at Vancouver Road. Work in Forward Area consisted of:- Revetting and clearing debris on N.E. I. Post. Front line fire steps in New Brunswick Trench and fire steps and equipment niches on Canada Trench. Fixing gas curtains and frames to dugouts on Left Brigade area. Work in Back Area consisted of:- Gun Post Store at Roclincourt and erecting Bessey Nissen huts for 243rd Machine Gun Coy. Making and painting sign boards etc for incoming forward area. Re-fitting sleeping apartments in Church Army Hut at Ecurie Cross Roads, completing canteen at Mont St Eloi. Forward Sections erecting small English Shelters on Canada Trench.	
"	24th		94th Brigade Canteen at Ecurie. Work continued on gun post store at Roclincourt, Nissen huts for 243rd M.G. Coy.	
"	26th		Fitting out 94th Brigade Canteen at Ecurie. Work continued on gun post store at Roclincourt, Nissen Huts for 243rd M.G. Coy. Conveying material to forward dumps etc.	

WAR DIARY of 211 Field Coy R.E.

Army Form C. 2118.

INTELLIGENCE SUMMARY.

(Erase heading not required.)

Place	Date	Hour	Summary of Events and Information	Remarks and references to Appendices
ECURIS	1917 DECEMBER 27TH		Forming Camp at DAYLIGHT RAILHEAD (CURRAGH CAMP) for one Company	
"	28TH		CAPT. G.T. POUND. R.E returned from FORWARD AREA. Forward section renovating N°2 Post Front Line. Repairing Dug-outs in trenches etc.	
"	29TH		MAJOR R.A.S. MAYSEL R.E. to FIRST ARMY School of instruction. BLENDEQUE	
"	31ST		CAPTAIN G.T. POUND R.E. " " " HARDELOT	
"			CAPTAIN F.W. MOORE M.C. R.E. of 223RD FIELD COY. R.E. acting as O.C. Company	

Attached Capt R.E.
a/c 211 Field Coy R.E.

WAR DIARY

OF THE

211TH FIELD COMPANY R.E.

From 1st Jan'y 1918 To 31st Jan 1918

Volume XXV

(ORIGINAL)

WAR DIARY
INTELLIGENCE SUMMARY
(Erase heading not required.)

Army Form C. 2118.

Instructions regarding War Diaries and Intelligence Summaries are contained in F. S. Regs., Part II. and the Staff Manual respectively. Title pages will be prepared in manuscript.

of the 211th Field Coy R.E.

Place	Date	Hour	Summary of Events and Information	Remarks and references to Appendices
ECURIE	January 1918 1st		No 4 Section from Coy. Camp. under Lieut. CALDECOTT, 11th EAST YORKS REGT attached 211th FIELD COY R.E. relieved No 2 Section in forward billets VANCOUVER ROAD. The forward work consisted of erecting gas curtain to dug outs, clearing trenches, fixing equipment nails and ammunition boxes, building ENGLISH Shelter in trenches, erecting gassed clothing and changing room at No 1 ST E.W. Rear work consisted of loading stores for Forward Dumps, fitting up canteen at CURRAGH CAMP, preparing ammunition box recesses for use in front line etc.	
"	2nd		opening and extending CURRAGH CAMP. CAPT HORSPOOL returned from leave. SHEFFIELD STRONG POINT at T.27.d.65.30 and BARNSLEY S.P. at T.27.d.60.65 commenced. Work in trench area continued.	
"	3rd		CAPT MOORE 223rd FIELD COY R.E. acting O.C. during absence of CAPT HORSPOOL and MAJOR MORSES handed duties over to CAPT HORSPOOL. Work continued as above in FORWARD and REAR area.	
"	4th		Work as in previous days	
"	5th		Commenced laying tramway track in order to transport material from the HORSE LINES of the 210th 211th and 223rd FIELD COYS to the manure dump. Making sign boards for trenches and painting notice boards for forward area. Repairing huts at CURAT CAMP. NEUVILLE ST VAAST. Work in forward area continued. C.S.M JOHN'S E.H awarded D.C.M on New Years Honours List.	
"	6th		Sunday. Work continued in forward area only.	
"	7th		Commenced excavating for new 94th BDE HQRS at B.14.a.7.3. BRIARY HILL. Work in Rear area continued	
"	8th		Work as on day before.	

Army Form C. 2118.

WAR DIARY
of THE 211TH FIELD Coy R.E.
INTELLIGENCE SUMMARY.
(Erase heading not required.)

Instructions regarding War Diaries and Intelligence Summaries are contained in F. S. Regs., Part II. and the Staff Manual respectively. Title pages will be prepared in manuscript.

Place	Date	Hour	Summary of Events and Information	Remarks and references to Appendices
ECURIE	January 1918 9th		No 2 Section went to forward billets under 2 Lieut Bush R.E. and 2 Lieut Winfield R.E. No 3 Section and 2 Lieut Fisher R.E came back to near billets. Capt Chalmers R.E. attached to this Coy for instruction left to join the 208th Field Coy R.E. Continued work on New Bde Hqrs, Currach Camp and on Brick area	
"	10th		Repairing Nissen huts in Springvale Camp, stoves etc in Ecuris Wood Camp on Brick area and continued work on New Bde Hqrs and Currach Camp in forward area.	
"	11th		Fixing Artillery sledges over Ottawa Trench in forward area. Bde Hqrs, and S.Ps continued. Work in back area continued on Ecuris, Springvale, and Cubit Camps, repairing etc.	
"	12th		Work continued as day before.	
"	13th		Work continued as day before by forward sections only (Sunday)	
"	14th		Repairing camps in back area continued. Commenced wiring Sheffield and Barnsley Strong Points	
"	15th		No 3 Section under 2 Lieut Fisher R.E went forward to Long Wood to assist 210th Field Coy in wiring trenches. Work on back area as on day before.	
"	16th		Repairs commenced to Boys Store. Vancouver R.E. Work continued on New Bde Hqrs. Strong Points, wiring etc in forward area and the repair of better area camps in back area.	
"	17th		Work as day before.	
"	18th		Major Mansel R.E. O.C. Coy. went on leave to U.K. from First Army School. Blendecques. Work in forward area and in back area continued as on day before.	

2353 Wt. W2544/1454 700,000 5/15 D. D. & L. A.D.S.S./Forms/C. 2118.

Army Form C. 2118.

WAR DIARY
OF THE 211TH FIELD COY R.E.
INTELLIGENCE SUMMARY.

(Erase heading not required.)

Instructions regarding War Diaries and Intelligence Summaries are contained in F. S. Regs., Part II. and the Staff Manual respectively. Title pages will be prepared in manuscript.

Place	Date	Hour	Summary of Events and Information	Remarks and references to Appendices
ECURIE	January 1918 19th		Work continued on forward area on Strong Points, New Bde Hqrs, Wiring Trenches etc. and on back area on Ecurie, Springvale, Cubit, and Cable Camps, repairing huts and stoves.	
"	20th		2 Lieut WINFIELD R.E. returned to new camp and N° 1 Section. 2 Lieut BURFIELD R.E. in charge. Went to forward billets. N° 4 Section moved back to the Gun Pits at Farbus to convert to NEW BRIGADE HEADQUARTERS at BRIERLY HILL. Commenced work on Bradford Strong Point at T.27.d.7.7.	
"	21st		Commenced excavation for new chamber to DRESSING STATION, VANCOUVER R^D. 2 Lieut FISHER R.E. returned with N° 3 Section to Coy Camp	
"	22nd		Work continued on forward area on New Bde Hqrs, Strong Points etc and on back area repairing huts in camps, Gum Boot Store at Roclincourt making and painting signs etc.	
"	23rd		Work as on day before.	
"	24th		Work as on day before.	
"	25th		Work in forward area continued. Repairing Nissen huts in back area continued. Commenced erecting hut for coal briquette at ROCLINCOURT	
"	26th		2 Lieut BUSH R.E. and N° 2 Section returned to camp. Lt CALDECOTT attached 211th Field Coy R.E. went to forward billets with N° 3 Section	
"	27th		SUNDAY. Work continued in forward area only	

2353 Wt. W3544/1454 700,000 5/15 D. D. & L. A.D.S.S./Forms/C. 2118.

Army Form C. 2118.

WAR DIARY
of
The 2/1st Field Coy. R.E.
INTELLIGENCE SUMMARY.
(Erase heading not required.)

Instructions regarding War Diaries and Intelligence Summaries are contained in F. S. Regs., Part II. and the Staff Manual respectively. Title pages will be prepared in manuscript.

Place	Date	Hour	Summary of Events and Information	Remarks and references to Appendices
ECURIE	January 1915 28th		Work continued as on day before in forward area. Completed Briquette Hutment Regincourt. Repairing and fixing stoves in Ecurie, Ecurie Railhead, H.Q. Divl Train and No 3 Divl Train camps on head area. Repairing huts and erecting coathooks on Cusit Camp continued.	
"	29th		Work as on day before.	
"	30th		Commenced work on Beehive Strong Point at T.27.d.3.7.	
"	31st		Work as on day before.	

F. Hoyden Capt R.E.
O.C. 2/1 [illegible] Engineers

Vol 24

WAR DIARY
OF
211TH FIELD COMPANY R.E.

FROM 1ST FEB 1918 TO 28TH FEB 1918

VOLUME XXVI

(ORIGINAL)

WAR DIARY of 211th Works Coy R.E.
INTELLIGENCE SUMMARY
(Erase heading not required.)

Army Form C. 2118.

Place	Date	Hour	Summary of Events and Information	Remarks and references to Appendices
ECURIE.	July 1918 1st		Nos. 1 & 3 Sections working in forward area, repairing and fixing shires also repairs on Aero Brigade HQrs at BRIERLEY HILL. No. 2 Section working in Courts. No 4 working Anzin area Supernumeraries afrest. 11 AM F.L.PARKIN joined Coy as	
	2nd		Work as day before. O/C MAJOR R.A.S MANSEL returned from leave and took up duties of A/CRE.	
	3rd		Work in forward area and on BRIERLEY HILL as day before. CAPT G.T. POUND (SUNDAY) to 86th Field Coy R.E. 20 O.R. of No. 2 Section on work at BRIERLEY HILL in addition to No 4 Section Remainder of No 1 Section on work in town.	
	4th		Work as day before. 11 a.m. H.W. BUSH & J.R.ES.FISHER relieves LIEUT. BURFIELD & LT.D.C. & L. SCOTT in forward area.	
	5th		Work as day before with the addition of forming town shops in Ecurie.	
	6th		Work as day before. 11 LT. F.R. BURFIELD went on leave.	
	7th		Work as day before.	(SUNDAY)
	8th		Work as day before.	
	9th		Work as day before.	
	10th		Work as day before. Work on rear area as usual. LT D/a COLESCOTT to ENGLAND for R.E. duties at DEGANWY. No. 2 Section relieves No 1 Section on work in forward area. Work as day before.	
	11th		432 JACKSON wounded by shell in forward area. Work as day before.	
	12th		Work as day before.	
	13th		Work as day before with the addition in the forward area of work on a new S.P. "FOVANT" B.3.a.7.0.	(SUNDAY)
	14th			

2353 Wt. W2544/1454 700,000 5/15 D.D.&L. A.D.S.S./Forms/C. 2118.

Army Form C. 2118.

WAR DIARY of 2/1st Field Coy RE

INTELLIGENCE SUMMARY.
(Erase heading not required.)

Instructions regarding War Diaries and Intelligence Summaries are contained in F.S. Regs., Part II and the Staff Manual respectively. Title pages will be prepared in manuscript.

Place	Date	Hour	Summary of Events and Information	Remarks and references to Appendices
ECURIE	Feb 1918 15th		Work as day before. 2nd Lt F.L. PARKIN relieved 2nd Lt H.W. BUSH in forward area.	
	16th		2nd Lt H.W. BUSH to Heavy Bridging Course at AIRE. No 1 Section relieved No 3 Section on work in forward area. Work as day before.	
	17th		Work as day before.	
	18th		Work as day before.	
	19th		Work as day before.	
	20th		Work as day before.	
	21st		Work as day before.	
	22nd		2nd Lt F.R. BURFIELD returned from leave. Work as day before.	
	23rd		Work as day before.	
	24th		Work as day before except on BRIERLEY HILL. Shells at LONG WOOD. 2nd Lt F.R. BURFIELD returned in forward area. 2nd Lt J.E. WINFIELD went on leave. 2nd Lt FISHER on work. Work as day before. Built the additional grounds on BRIERLEY HILL	
	25th		No 3 Section relieved No 4 Section on BRIERLEY HILL. Work as day before.	
	26th		Work as day before except No 4 Section were cleaning vehicles + packing transport.	
	27th			
	28th		Nos 1 & 2 Sections returned to camp - being relieved by 2 Sections of 457th Coy RE in town, remainder of Coy packing up and preparing for Coy move. 2nd Lt F.R. BURFIELD + 2nd Lt F.L. PARKIN remained in forward area to hand over work.	

M W Munro Major
OC 2/1st Field Coy RE

31st Divisional Engineers

WAR DIARY

211th FIELD COMPANY   R.E.

MARCH 1918

ORIGINAL.

CONFIDENTIAL.

WAR DIARY
of
211th Field Company.R.E.

From 1/3/18 to 31/3/18.

VOLUME XVII

WAR DIARY

211th Field Coy R.E.

INTELLIGENCE SUMMARY

Army Form C. 2118

Place	Date March	Hour	Summary of Events and Information	Remarks and references to Appendices
ECURIE	1/3/18	—	Company paraded at 9 am and marched to MAREUIL and sub-billets. Three 2/Lts F.R. BURFIELD & F.L. PARKIN reporting for duty at 8 am and 5 pm respectively to take over work.	
MAREUIL	2nd		Nos. 1 + 3 Sections under 2/Lt. F.R./BURFIELD & RE FISHER supervising work of 5th Rehoboth Bn. Wry covering ladders XIII Corps Defence School BERTONVAL & ST AUBIN Cue. Nos. 2 + 4 Sections unloading transport and repairing huts & NISSEN HUTS.	
"	3rd		Work as day before.	
"	4th		Nos. 1 + 3 Section work as day before with the addition of No. 4 Section under 2/Lt F.L. PARKIN. No. 2 Section loading transport and moving Coy field stores to BRUNEHAUT FARM Camp. Remainder Section remaining at MAREUIL.	
BRUNEHAUT FARM	5th		Nos. 1, 3, 4 & Sections work as day before. No. 2 Section working on trenching & a new Camp. C.S.M. E.H. JOHNS D.C.M. went on leave. O/C Major R.S. MAURSSR reporting Coy.	
"	6th		Work as day before. No. 2 Section also on making temporary sign boards to Brunehaut Volume.	
"	7th		Work as day before.	
"	8th		Work as day before.	
"	9th		Work as day before. 400 Chinese digging dugouts at BRUNEHAUT POST F 23 c 2.2. Summer time came into operation at 11 pm.	
"	10th		Work as day before. 200 Chinese digging trench at " " "	
"	11th		Work as day before but only 1 Coy of 4th Brehant. Battn at PILLAR POST F 17 a 1.5; TERRIER POST F 23 a 3.7 & BRUNEHAUT POST F 23 C 2.2. 130, 196 + 30 Chinese respectively digging & trenches. Coy moved into billets at MAREUIL.	
MAREUIL	12th		Work as day before with the exception of Chinese Labour. 2/Lt J E WINFIELD returned from leave.	

Army Form C. 2118.

WAR DIARY of 211th Field Coy RE
INTELLIGENCE SUMMARY.
(Erase heading not required.)

Instructions regarding War Diaries and Intelligence Summaries are contained in F. S. Regs., Part II and the Staff Manual respectively. Title pages will be prepared in manuscript.

Place	Date March/18	Hour	Summary of Events and Information	Remarks and references to Appendices
MAREUIL	13th		Work as day before. with the addition grinding cinders for furnace.	
"	14th		Work as day before. L.G. Instructor from 13th K.O.Yr.L.I. starting duties. 1/C RES FISHER went on leave.	
"	15th		Work as day before. Making of Cinders on paths. 2 Coys 2 & 4th Infantry Batty on work with conveniences at THANKERDEAR POST 62 B.O.R'S	
"	16th		Work as day before.	
"	17th		Work as day before. with the addition of work on VASE POST E 18 9. Battery equipment handed over to MI PortorPuke R.E.	
"	18th		Work as day before.	
"	19th		Work as day before.	
"	20th		Work as day before.	
"	21st		Work as day before.	
"	22nd		12.15 a.m. orders to move were received. Coy paraded at 7 a.m. and left by Buses at 8 a.m. to 1 mile W. of SAVY and thence to BLAIREVILLE reaching there about 11 a.m. Transport under CAPT HORSPOOL - left at 10 a.m. for BASSEUX where they were ordered to BLAIREVILLE which was reached at 10.45 p.m. Whole Coy billeted in MINES & FRENCH huts at BLAIREVILLE.	

WAR DIARY
INTELLIGENCE SUMMARY.
(Erase heading not required.)

Army Form C. 2118.

Instructions regarding War Diaries and Intelligence Summaries are contained in F.S. Regs, Part II and the Staff Manual respectively. Title pages will be prepared in manuscript.

Place	Date	Hour	Summary of Events and Information	Remarks and references to Appendices
BLARGICOURT	23rd		O/C and 4 section officers & Lts F.R. BUFFIELD, R.W. BUSH, R.L. PARKIN & J.E. WINFIELD left at 6 am to reconnoitre trench system N. of HAVRINCOURT at 3 pm CAPT. HOWARD went forward at 30.a.75.60 and returned about 1.30 about and found suitable for HQ at ECHELLES-LE-COMTE at A14.b.1.2. "L" WINFIELD & Co went forward to billet area sheet 57BNW ST E N.W. as O/C 7/250 Advance Party for demolition dumbelle NW sheet 57BNW.	
COURCELLES LE COMTE	24th 1940		O/C and Nos 1, 2 & 3 Section Officers & Lts BUFFIELD, BUSH, PARKIN went thro' area forming up enemi and marked L.H. and R.H. sectors i.e. at COURCELLES battery A10.0.5.8. and A16. central - Ref sheet 57D N.W. each middle of A14.b.90. attach return CAPT HICKSON remaining to same bridge, at 1.30 am the 2 and sections Co marched to rendezvous A9.d.35.0 and at 4.15 am 4 sections reported to Coy HQ at his takers (CAPT. HOWARD) and waited for N 55 Div mans. Sappers worked on tanks F4.a.2.B. reaching main 9.30 am and by 3.15 pm 1-2nd transport route up about 5 hour and ¾ 3rd worked up at W. 30. C. 7. 2. to find E.P. MOUTRY as Bks 5.30 am. He and all transport left for billet area (B. Camp) out lest trunks had gone. Section left camp by 7-8 am and 57D.	
	25th		A.2.0. A.0.6. Ref Sheet 57D N.W. 5TP and 57D	
MOYENEVILLE E.6.a.7.8	26th		about 5 am Coy officers transport CRE being impt, 2nd MOSTYN took over from LINK. Bn by 9am CAPT HOWARD 25.a./ 29.a went ahead and began laid to RHQ MOYENVILLE 40 pags then 9am all and arrived at W 30.C.7 2 am about 57D.	
	27th		at 9am O/O & O/C and 11th T. BUFFIELD, BUSH & PARKIN and (recce) reconnoiter BURBLE LINE from X22.5.9.0. 5 to the F149 subsector 57D.	

WAR DIARY
INTELLIGENCE SUMMARY

of 211th Field Coy R.E.

Army Form C. 2118.

(Erase heading not required.)

Place	Date	Hour	Summary of Events and Information	Remarks and references to Appendices
	1918 March 27th (Contd.)		At 4. & 11. Lt BURFIELD between 4.30 a.m. & 6 a.m. pegged out purple line from about F.8.b.7.5. to about E.8.d.7.6. at the left of Keux & relieved 11 Lt. BUSH and PARKIN returned to dug out same. Coy carried out orders received for N.30 from MAJOR SPEIGHT of 210th Field Coy R.E. that the Coy was to hold PURPLE LINE time to bring up their field magnet, S.A.A. of the Coy was moved by wago[n] to the R.E. dump and dug in about X.22.d.0.4. & X.28.a.4.7. & dawn. He Coy was ordered by the 10th E.Y.R. 4.30 am to withdraw from X.22.d.0.4. & X.28.a.4.7. At 6 a.m. Coy (worrd & Rgt H.Q's) withdrew to E.5.a.3.9. H.Q's & unit H.Q's. At 8 a.m. (transport Parks) and to unit H.Q's. " E.l.b.6.2. via BERLES & POMMIER	
	28th		At dawn Coy withdrew through ADINFER and Autoplates at X.26.a.3.3. at 8.30 a.m. orders were received from Brigadier BAZTONIER Brigade H.Q. at the Coy was to Man and Hold at wall across PURPLE LINE at F.8.c. BURFIELD Coy reached this position about 9.30 a.m. During afternoon a party 11 Lt BURFIELD reconnoitred line to be held between F.14.b.6.0 and F.18.d.5.3. This line was used at night by Nos 1, 2 & 3 sections.	
	29th		At dawn Coy was relieved by 11th E. LANCS R. and withdrew to the dry bed of Rgt COJEUL RIVER F.2.C.5.1. After a meal Coy was ordered to act as support to 10th E.Y.R. of Bn reports to C/O of Battn at X.27.d.2.7. and was ordered to post the Coy in ADINFER WOOD at X.27.C.8.8. 3 casualties during the night from shrapnel fire.	X.27 d.28.5 F.2 d.82.
	30th		At dawn a/c & 11 Lt's BURFIELD (BUSH & PARKIN) reconnoitred & pegged out line of wire along whole Battn front from X.27 d.28.5 F.2 d.82. At 11 a.m. Coy was ordered to F.2.C.5.1 to act as support to the right flank of the Battn. 10th & 28th section under 11 Lt PARKIN headquarters stirs & trans[port] dumps for wiring	
	31st		Between 2 am and 4 am No's 1, 2 + 3 sections under 11 Lt's BURFIELD + PARKIN erected wiring noving trench knife fence alongs the right flank of the Battn front from F.2 d.82. G F.3. a.3.5. At 8 a.m. Transport & H.Qs withdrew to ST AMANT.	

2353 Wt. W2544/1454 700,000 5/15 D.D.&L. A.D.S.S./Forms/C. 2118.

WAR DIARY of 211th Field Coy R.E.

Army Form C. 2118.

Place	Date	Hour	Summary of Events and Information	Remarks and references to Appendices
	March 1918 31st (Cont)	At 5.35 p.m. Coy was relieved by the 208th Field Coy R.E. and marched to the W. side of MONCHY-AU-BOIS and was thence taken to billets in ST AMAND on Coy transport. Map reference - Sheets 51C & 57D.	

H Horbot
Capt RE
a/c 211th Field Coy R.E.

31st Divisional Engineers

211st FIELD COMPANY R.E. ::: APRIL 1918.

ORIGINAL.

CONFIDENTIAL.

WAR DIARY

of

211th Field Company.R.E.

From April 1st to April 30th, 1918.

VOLUME XXVIII

Army Form C. 2118.

WAR DIARY of 211th Field Coy R.E.
INTELLIGENCE SUMMARY
(Erase heading not required.)

Instructions regarding War Diaries and Intelligence Summaries are contained in F. S. Regs., Part II. and the Staff Manual respectively. Title pages will be prepared in manuscript.

Place	Date April 1918	Hour	Summary of Events and Information	Remarks and references to Appendices
ST AMANT	1st	6.30 a.m.	Lt. WINFIELD left to recce fields at BAUDRICOURT.	
		1 p.m.	Coy paraded and marched off being unfortunately billeted at SUS ST LEGER.	
SUS.ST.LEGER	2nd	7 a.m.	Lt. WINFIELD left to gr fields at MARQUAY.	
		8.30 a.m.	Coy paraded and marched to LIENCOURT where it entrained and was taken via FREVENT & ST POL to LA BELLE EPINE. As early place of detrained & marched to MARQUAY into fields at 2 p.m.	
		9 a.m.	Transport all under Lt. BURFIELD for MARQUAY.	
			Overhauling Kit, equipment & Tool Carts &c. Lt. R.E.S. FISHER rejoins Coy from leave.	
MARQUAY	3rd		"	
"	4th		Coy at Physical Training. Squad Drill incl. arms. Gas drill and instruction	
"	5th		of Lewis gun. Attended critic drill. Final prep to	
"	6th		Work as day before	
"	7th		Work as day before	
"	8th		Work as day before	
"	9th		Work as day before. O.C. MAJOR MANSEL rejoined Coy.	
"	10th		Reconnoitres new ground at 4.30 p.m. and marched off and entrained on the BRYAS-SIEVAL Rd about 6 p.m. Transport & HQ left at 5.30 p.m.	
VIEUX BERQUIN	11th		Coy bus transport + HQ arrived 3 a.m. & machine at night moved about 1500 S.E. of BLEU. Transport + HQs arrived at ECQUEDECQUES at 2 a.m. and left at 9 a.m. and arrived at BORRE at 7 p.m.	

2353 Wt. W2544/1454 700,000 5/15 D.D. & L. A.D.S.S./Forms/C. 2118.

WAR DIARY

INTELLIGENCE SUMMARY

of the 211th Field Coy R.E.

Army Form C. 2118.

Place	Date April	Hour	Summary of Events and Information	Remarks and references to Appendices
VIEUX-BERQUIN	12th		About midday No 3 Section Billet was struck by a shell. Sapper COPLEY was killed and Sergt MAWSON, L/C BEE & Sappers BARNETT, LYON & LYMAN were wounded. Owing to the retirement of the infantry the Coy was ordered back to MERRIS. On arrival at MERRIS about five Depanis were thrown during by at MERRIS. L/C SWIFT and SAPPER JACKSON were wounded. The Coy and 223rd/Field Coy were apparently reported to Lt.Col. GURNEY A.S.O. who was in Command of the Infantry. The two Field Coys 92" Pompne T.M.B. and some Stragglers occupied a defensive line at NORA HOLF (S.E. of STRAZEELE) and remained there until about 3am dug in.	
HONDEGHEM	13th		The Coy was relieved in the trenches by the 1st Australian Engineers and marched into Camps of the 1st Australian Transport withdrew from BORRE to about Camp about 8.30 am. South of HONDEGHEM.	
"	14th		Overhauling lost Carts &c.	
"	15th		Work as day before.	
"	16th		Work as day before.	
"	17th		Coy worked digging trenches on the HAZEBROUCK defences from LA KREULE running S to the HAZEBROUCK-BAILLEUL Rd.	
"	18th		Work as day before.	
"	19th		Company were paraded at 9.30 am, and marched into Billets at AD SOUVERAIN. About 7am No 3 Section Billet was struck by a shell. L/C OAKLEY & SAPPER TOWN were killed and SAPPER LAWRENCE died of wounds. A/Sergt. BARRETT, 2nd Corpl. FRIEND & HOLMES, SAPPERS SWIFT, TOMSETT, ARCHIBALD, EDWARDS, HAINSWORTH & WILSON and PIONEERS FOZZARA & JANSON were wounded. The Coy were then moved into Billets N of LE TIR ANGLAIS. Transport moved at 10am to LA CUNEVELE.	

Army Form C. 2118.

WAR DIARY
of the 211th (1st Feld) Coy R.E.

INTELLIGENCE SUMMARY.
(Erase heading not required.)

Instructions regarding War Diaries and Intelligence Summaries are contained in F. S. Regs., Part II and the Staff Manual respectively. Title pages will be prepared in manuscript.

Place	Date April	Hour	Summary of Events and Information	Remarks and references to Appendices
LE TIR ANGLAIS	20th		Coy on improvement and wiring support line from PETIT SEC BOIS to BOIS D'AVAL and front trench at Cross roads and no bridges.	
"	21st		Work as day before.	
"	22nd		Work as day before. SAPPER GRIFFITHS was wounded at LE TIR ANGLAIS	
"	23rd		Work as day before	
"	24th		Work as day before. Sapper MAKINSON was wounded at SWARTENBROUCK.	
"	25th		Work as day before.	
"	26th		Work as day before.	
"	27th		About 10 am Coy paraded and marched to trenches at LES CISEAUX. Transport also moved there at 11 am.	
LES CISEAUX	28th		Coy unloading with carts. equipment and gas drills.	
"	29th		Coy on work on "D" line HAZEBROUCK. defences from LAKREULE running S to the HAZEBROUCK. BAILLEUL Rd. consists of revetments and wiring to Work on any type.	
"	30th			

Hosptl Coy RE
11/c 211(1st) Coy RE

ORIGINAL.

CONFIDENTIAL.

WAR DIARY

of

211th Field Company. R.E.

From 1/5/18 to 31/5/18.

VOLUME ~~III~~ XX/X

WAR DIARY of the 211th Field Coy R.E.

INTELLIGENCE SUMMARY

Army Form C. 2118

Place	Date	Hour	Summary of Events and Information	Remarks and references to Appendices
LES CISEAUX	Aug 1st		Coy at work on the HAZEBROUCK - BAILLEUL Rly henches evening supervising working parties. in KREUNE & S. HAZEBROUCK defences, wiring, engineers and R.E.(?)	
"	2nd		Work as day before.	
"	3rd		Work as day before.	
"	4th		Work as day before.	
"	5th		Work as day before.	
"	6th		Work as before.	
"	7th		Work as day before.	
"	8th		Work as day before.	
"	9th		Nos 2, 3 & 4 Sections moved forward to finish shelters at MT NOIR for work on Reserve Line. ROUKLOSHILLE trench & THÊTRE defences. No 1 Section on leave gun shelter digging and preparing wiring materials for 3 forward sections.	
"	10th		Work as day before.	
"	11th		Work as day before.	
"	12th		Work as day before.	
"	13th		Work as day before.	

Army Form C. 2118.

WAR DIARY
of the 2/1st (Res) Coy RE

INTELLIGENCE SUMMARY.
(Erase heading not required.)

Instructions regarding War Diaries and Intelligence Summaries are contained in F. S. Regs., Part II. and the Staff Manual respectively. Title pages will be prepared in manuscript.

Place	Date	Hour	Summary of Events and Information	Remarks and references to Appendices
LES CISEAUX	May 14th		No 1 Section went forward, the 2 2nd Lt Inglis returned to camp. Work as day time and the exception of that at Coy camp.	
"	15th		Work as day time. No 2 Section on leave. 5 men working on theory and pigeon wiring methods for 3 forward stations. 2 Lt RES FISHER opened horse stomech.	
"	16th	16.00	Work as day time except that No 1 section now took up work of runners from 0ffices of Fd0.	
"	17th		Work as day to the with the addition of work at Horse Station doing repairs by No 2 Section.	
"	18th		Work as day to the.	
"	19th		Work as day to the.	
"	20th		No 2 Section was performed to 80.4 Section runners to camp. Work as day time with the exception of that at Coy Camp.	
"	21st		Work as day to the.	
"	22nd		Work as day to the. 2 Lt RES returned Coy	
"	23rd		Work as day to the. 2 Lt J.E WINFIELD & Lieut HAIG (for ORIEL) proceeded to RE Depot to report 2 Lt RES FISHER any party Chalke went on in advance at 7 am & Lts met field from 63rd Fd Coy RE. Lt Hurton & Duboire for General & 3 vehicles and marched to LA BRESLE entraining. First unit a trail to 3 vehicles HEURINGHEM arrived about 9 pm. Transport persons and 3 bus her marked HEURINGHEM where was a total entry of 3.30am.	
HEURINGHEM	24th			

Army Form C. 2118.

WAR DIARY

of the 2/1st Field Coy RE

INTELLIGENCE SUMMARY

(Erase heading not required.)

Place	Date	Hour	Summary of Events and Information	Remarks and references to Appendices
HELRINGHEM	May 23rd		Infantry and artillery out in the fields	
"	26.		2 Lt BURFIELD & No 1 Section moved to LUMBRES at 8.30am to work on Second Brigade brigade fields. Church Service P.C. 7.45 am. C.O.'s 10am	
"	27.		Nos 2, 3, 4 Sections on P.T. Musketry & leather drill with armed and games.	
"	28.		Nos 2, 3, 4 Sections continued. Company Training.	
"	29.		Work as day before with the addition of leaving horse-post for G.O.C. inspection	
"	30.		Work as day before. 2 Lt JEWINGSTER rejoins Coy	
"	31.		Coy less transport entrained at 7am for QUERNES for advance & ceremonial parade with 93rd Infantry Brigade. returning to billets about 2pm.	

J Husset Capt RE
for O/C 2/1st Lond Coy RE

WAR DIARY
OF THE
211TH FIELD COMPANY R.E.

FROM 1ST JUNE 1918 TO 30TH JUNE 1918

VOLUME XX

(ORIGINAL)

WAR DIARY

INTELLIGENCE SUMMARY.

(Erase heading not required.)

Army Form C. 2118.

of ...... 2/1st 2nd Coy R.E.

Place	Date	Hour	Summary of Events and Information	Remarks and references to Appendices
HEURINGHEM	June 1st		Transport turned at 5am and moved to Yds AT LUMBRES and was met by the R.B.C. at 11am. The remaining half of Coy turned at 8.30 am and detrained at HEURINGHEN. Chaining at 12 noon proceed to QUELMES where it was joined by Mo1 Section. This then the good of advance parade of two companies of the R.E. and of the second half of Military Cross. No1 Section composed parade at about 50% of Coy were inoculated at 9.15 am	
"	2nd		There not inoculated continued Coy training.	
"	3rd		Work as day before.	
"	4th		Work as day before.	
"	5th		Work as day before.	
"	6th		Work as day before.	
"	7th		Work as day before.	
"	8th		Divisional R.E. Rifle meeting. No Coy parades in the date.	
"	9th		Sunday. No Coy parades on this date.	
"	10th		Divisional R.E. Sports (ARELCHE). No Coy parade on this date.	
"	11th		Coy training.	
"	12th		Coy training & kit in the reporalis.	
"	13th		Coy training. Whole of Coy Transport inspected by C.R.E. CAPT F. HORSFORD went on leave.	

Army Form C. 2118.

WAR DIARY of 2/11th Field Coy R.E.

INTELLIGENCE SUMMARY.

(Erase heading not required.)

Instructions regarding War Diaries and Intelligence Summaries are contained in F. S. Regs., Part II. and the Staff Manual respectively. Title pages will be prepared in manuscript.

Place	Date	Hour	Summary of Events and Information	Remarks and references to Appendices
HEURINCHEM	June 14th		Nos 1 & 2 Sections finishing at CANAL near BLARINGHEM. No 3 & 4 Sections training & inspection of kit & equipment.	
"	15th		Coy paraded at 12.35 p.m. and marched to U.17.67.8 S of STAPLE arriving at 6.30 p.m. and bivouacked for the night.	
U.17.6.7.8	16th		Coy stood by.	
"	17th		Coy paraded at 4.35 p.m. and marched to RACQUINGHEM and went into billets.	
RACQUINGHEM	18th		Coy carrying out improvements to billets and off-loading pontoons & tools & equipment at Canal near BLARINGHEM.	
"	19th		Coy training.	
"	20th		Coy paraded at 3.15 p.m. and marched to C.6.b.1.1 E of SPERCQ and encamped.	
C.6.a.11.	21st		At Camp. Sections Officers & Section Serjts (cycles) journey to RR rly work & billets Nr 570th Field Coy RE. At 2 p.m. detachments men of Coy (on foot and march) Nos. 1, 2 & 3 Sections to billets at D.9.C.6.3 & No 4 Section to billets at D.3.b.5.5. Transport under L.T J.E.WYFIELD moved off at 3.35 p.m. and arrived at 7.25 p.m. arrived at 4.30 p.m. and camped there.	
D.9.C.6.3	22nd		Coy improving billets & camp and settling in.	
"	23rd		Coy on work on tramways, new crossings of Enghien-Arras tramways, bridges on Pebilley bicks, inspecting running and dumps, Arthuey Breastworks, erecting Enguard & battens, Crossbars, hedges & preparing blueprints for muletracks etc.	

Army Form C. 2118.

WAR DIARY
of 2/11th Field Coy R.E.
INTELLIGENCE SUMMARY.
(Erase heading not required.)

Instructions regarding War Diaries and Intelligence Summaries are contained in F.S. Regs., Part II. and the Staff Manual respectively. Title pages will be prepared in manuscript.

Place	Date	Hour	Summary of Events and Information	Remarks and references to Appendices
B.P.C.63.	June 24th		Work as day before.	
"	25th		Work as day before.	
"	26th		Work as day before.	
"	27th		Work as day before.	
"	28th		Nos 1, 2 & 3 Sections together with 2 Sections of the 2/10th Fld Coy R.E. took part in the operations on this date. Anglo Cut gaps marked with distinguishing marks & wire trails for a mile thick from F.28.a.4.1 & F.29.a.7.5.10. No 2 Section under 2 Lt BURFIELD but down six exit widenews for a mile track from K.4 i.15 6 K.5.b.3.7. No 3 Section under 2 Lt FISHER completed trench Shiny Point at K.5.a.9.4. One NCO & 1 Sapper were wounded.	
"	29th		No 4 Section carried on work on Advanced Brigade H.Qs and inspection of trench.	
"	30th		Coy on work on Advanced Brigade HQs, erection of Enfilade Shelter, improving of Dennies, fixing gas curtains for shelters & improving & making notices trench. Same weather.	

3/7/18

H Newland Capt RE
O/C 2/11th Fd Coy RE

WAR DIARY

OF

211TH FIELD COMPANY R.E.

FROM 1st JULY 1918 TO 31st JULY 1918

VOLUME XXXI

(ORIGINAL)

Army Form C. 2118.

WAR DIARY

OF THE 2/1st FIELD Coy. R.E.

INTELLIGENCE SUMMARY.

(Erase heading not required.)

Instructions regarding War Diaries and Intelligence Summaries are contained in F. S. Regs., Part II. and the Staff Manual respectively. Title pages will be prepared in manuscript.

Place	Date	Hour	Summary of Events and Information	Remarks and references to Appendices
Dqe63 Sheet 36A	July 1918 1		Coy. on Work in Forward Area consisting of constructing & completing mines, facing gas curtains, making & painting revetting boards. Mounted Section & Transport at Horse Lines W.25.d.07 Sheet 27. Work on day before, with addition of work on Batt. H.Q. E.25.a S.6. D.24.c.7.1. E.20 & 51. Adv. Bttn. H.Q., Batt. H.Q. i/c g	
	2		"	
	3		"	
	4		" in addition this road mines prepared and blown.	
	5		"	
	6		" Capt. HORSPOOL 2/1st Coy. to Command 447 FIELD Coy. R.E.	
	7		"	
	8		"	
	9		"	
	10		"	
	11		Company Reserve Coy. — No. 3 Sec. under Lt. FISHER came down to TRANSPORT LINES for work in Back Area consisting of work on Div. H.Q., in moving Camp etc. — Nos. 1, 2 & 4 Secs. continued work on Right Batt. H.Q. E.25.d S.6., Batt. H.Q. E.20 & 51, painting, making & facing notice boards, facing gas curtains.	

/Capt. R.V.N. BUCHANAN posted to Unit vice CAPT. HORSPOOL

D.D. & L.

WAR DIARY

of THE 211TH FIELD COY. R.E.

INTELLIGENCE SUMMARY.

(Erase heading not required.)

Army Form C. 2118.

Place	Date	Hour	Summary of Events and Information	Remarks and references to Appendices
D9c63 Sheet 36A	July 1918			
	12		Work as day before, with addition of constructing C.R. for R.A. commenced.	
	13		" " " "	
	14		" " " "	
	15		" " 92nd Inf. Bd. Batts. instructed in Wiring, laying out Trenches, Sandbagging.	
			A/Capt. BUCHANAN left Unit & proceeded to ENGLAND on duty. Work on English	
			Gults for Div. Report Centre commenced.	
	16		Work as day before	
	17		" " " "	
	18		English Gults to Div. Report Centre completed.	
			1 Lieut. R.E.S. FISHER went to forward H.Q. & took over	
	19		from Major R.A.S. MANSEL. 92nd Inf. Bd. Batts instructed in Wiring, etc.	
	20		Work as day before, 92nd Inf. Bd. Batt. instruction on wiring.	
			Major R.A.S. MANSEL proceeded to ENGLAND on Special Leave.	
	21		Work as day before	
	22		" " " "	
	23		" " " "	

Army Form C. 2118.

WAR DIARY

of THE 211TH FIELD Coy. R.E.

INTELLIGENCE SUMMARY.

(Erase heading not required.)

Instructions regarding War Diaries and Intelligence Summaries are contained in F. S. Regs., Part II and the Staff Manual respectively. Title pages will be prepared in manuscript.

Place	Date	Hour	Summary of Events and Information	Remarks and references to Appendices
Dq0a3 Sht 36A	24		Work as day before.	
	25		"	
	26		"	
	27		"	
	28		"	
	29		1 Sapper Wounded.	
	30		"	
	31		"	

2nd Aug. 1918.

R.E.S. Hahn
Lieut. R.E.
O.C. 211th Field Coy. R.E.

WAR DIARY
of
211TH FIELD COMPANY R.E.

From August 1st To August 31st 1916

Volume XVII

(Original)

Vol 30

Army Form C. 2118.

WAR DIARY
or
INTELLIGENCE SUMMARY.
(Erase heading not required.)

Instructions regarding War Diaries and Intelligence Summaries are contained in F. S. Regs., Part II. and the Staff Manual respectively. Title pages will be prepared in manuscript.

Place	Date	Hour	Summary of Events and Information	Remarks and references to Appendices
Transport V.25.c.9.7. (Hut 27.) Forward D.9.c.6.4 (Hut 36a)	Aug. 1918. 1st.		Company in Reserve. 2nd Lt Fisher was a/O.C., No. 3 section was training at Transport Lines and working under 2nd Lt Winfield. No 4 section being under 2nd Lt Parker. The work in hand consisted of :— Forward. Left Battn H.Qrs. (E.20.b.53.10). Reinforced cement covered English shelter large the work being in progress. Reinforced cement block pill box, of which the floor was completed. Reserve Battn H.Qrs. (E.26.d.5.6). Sandbagging work and laying cement shelter cover. Regt. Aid Post. (E.25.d.4.8). Laying floor towards in shelter and constructing bridge at entrance. Lynods Shelter. (E.26.a.65.40). Sandbagging and fixing gas curtains to entrance. Adv. Regt. Centre. (D.18.b.9.7). Sandbagging. 124 Bgd. R.F.A. (D.18.d.9.7). Fixing gas curtain. 170 Bgd. R.F.A. (D.26.b.5.8). Erecting Elephant shelter large and clearing out bedding. Reinforcing cellar for R.A. (D.23.d.15.85). In hand. Sinking well for R.A. (C.24.a.05.30). Excavation in hand. Advanced Dressing Station. (D.9.d.1.8). Making brackets for stretchers.	

WAR DIARY or INTELLIGENCE SUMMARY

Place	Date	Hour	Summary of Events and Information	Remarks and references to Appendices
Rear.	Aug. 1st. (con)		Erecting Hut for Signals (D.H.Q. at V.30.c.1.6) In hand. Sinking well for No 2 Fd. Amb. Dis. Farm. (C.8.b.5.6) In hand. Making Forming Tables for A.D.M.S. at Transport Lines. Constructing tank-proofs to memo tanks and traverse round Hun standing yet. Transport Line.	
	2nd		Instructing Infantry in Wiring, Sandbagging, Laying out trenches etc. Demonstrating camouflage at RENESCURE commenced.	
	3rd		Repairing windows, fixing blinds &c at Bgd. HQrs, HAZEBROUCK. (V.27.c.3.2).	
	4th		Erecting Camouflage O.P. (E.28.c.3.3.44.)	
	5th		Blowing ebilling Bridge, BOIS DES HUIT RUES (C.12.a.4.5) Making Tent for water cart at water tanks at D.H.Q. (V.30.c.1.6)	
	6th		Lt. Blades joined Coy from 156th Fd. Coy. as second-in-command. Instructing Infantry in Wiring, Sandbagging, Laying out trenches etc. Sapper Newsom. G.E. killed in action.	
	8th		Fitting cellars at Bgd. Hqrs. HAZEBROUCK. (V.27.c.3.2).	

Army Form C. 2118.

WAR DIARY
or
INTELLIGENCE SUMMARY.
(Erase heading not required.)

Instructions regarding War Diaries and Intelligence Summaries are contained in F. S. Regs., Part II. and the Staff Manual respectively. Title pages will be prepared in manuscript.

Place	Date	Hour	Summary of Events and Information	Remarks and references to Appendices
	Aug 8th (cont.)		Repairing road at D.2.c.8.0 with lorries erected from HAZEBROUCK.	
	9th		Major Marvel, M.C., R.E. returned from leave to U.K. Reporting G.O.C. men making & fixing gutter to C.S.O.2.'s hut at D.H.Q. (V.30.c.1.6)	
	10th		Making three light mule track bridges in six sections for 121st Inft. Bgd.	
	11th		Relieved 210th Field Coy, taking over the fills at HAZEBROUCK GARAGE in neighbourhood of D.5.C.9.1. Captain Roach moved to forward billets from transport lines.	
	12th		Work in hand. Front Taken over from 210th Field Coy. Left Bgd H.Qrs. (E.20.b.53.10) Hut in cement felt box. Elephant Shelter 170 Bgd H.qrs. R.F.A. (E.16.a.0.7) Excavating for and erecting two shelters English model. (E.15.c.65.15) Erecting hurdles. (about E.21.a.) and puckling and wiring round Puckling Parapet of Brastwork (about E.15.a. to E.15.c.) and making out horseshoe Revetting Trench Z'Inn. (E.9.d.0.6)	
	13th		2nd Lieut Bush left on leave to U.K. 2nd Lieut Fisher left on leave to PARIS. Repairing road bridge (E.11.c.25.05).	

Army Form C. 2118.

WAR DIARY
or
INTELLIGENCE SUMMARY.
(Erase heading not required.)

Instructions regarding War Diaries and Intelligence Summaries are contained in F. S. Regs., Part II. and the Staff Manual respectively. Title pages will be prepared in manuscript.

Place	Date	Hour	Summary of Events and Information	Remarks and references to Appendices
	Aug 15th		Major Marvel. M.C., R.E. awarded bar to M.C.	
			2nd Lt. Fisher Rewarded M.C.	
			Sergt. C. of Hit M.M. R.E. awarded D.C.M.	
	19th 20th		All working parties cancelled owing to German retirement.	
	21st		Erecting timber bridge at E.20.b.4.4. crossing SWARTENBROUCK and "B" RIDE.	
	24th		Company moved out forward and war killets were taken over by the 22nd Field Coy R.E. 40th Div. The relieved the 65th Field Coy R.E., 9th Div. taking over war killets at P.36.b.75.05. (Sheet 21) and forward killets at Q.26.b.1.2 (Sheet 21)	
	25th		Work on forward camp to accommodate sections and officers leaving there. Enemy gas over X.Y.A.6.9.	
			Work in renewing X.2.b.0.5. and H. Perks returnent from Penn Farm.	
	29th		Sandbagging entrance to aid post X.2.d.6.9.	
	30th		Just Perks element from leave to U.K.	
	31st		Owing to German retirement Company moved forward to X.9.a.6.4. (sheet 27.) all sections and transport being at the "Brewery". the team working in refuses of shelters BAILLEUL	

COMMANDING
21ST FIELD COMPANY R.E.

ORIGINAL.

CONFIDENTIAL.

WAR DIARY

of

211th Field Company.R.E.

From 1st Sept. to 30th Sept. 1918.

~~VOLUME XXIX~~

Volume XXXIII

CONFIDENTIAL.

Army Form C. 2118.

WAR DIARY
or
INTELLIGENCE SUMMARY.
(Erase heading not required.)

Instructions regarding War Diaries and Intelligence Summaries are contained in F. S. Regs., Part II. and the Staff Manual respectively. Title pages will be prepared in manuscript.

Place	Date	Hour	Summary of Events and Information	Remarks and references to Appendices
	Sept.			
LA BESACE FARM. X.9.a.4.4. Sheet 27 S.E.	1st.		Work in hand consisted of clearing roads and filling in shell hits at BAILLEUL after the German retirement. Preparing for and carrying on station for the construction of heavy traffic bridge over stream at LA BARRIERE CALVERDANS (X.F.c.b.1.)	
	2nd		Preparing approaches and erection of winch ram. 2nd Lt. Fisher left to hunt for O.R. Enemy shells in own camp in addition to shop.	
Field at 5.27.c.8.6. (Sheet 28 S.W.)	5th		Company paraded at 6 a.m. and moved to S.27.C.T.6 near BAILLEUL-ARMENTIERS Road, arriving at 7.45 a.m. Off 1 p.m. No 1, 2 and 3 sections moved forward to T.25.a.0.2.	
	6th		Work began consisted of repairing road filling in shell hits in WATERLOO ROAD and WESTHOF ROAD. Salvaging timber for forming dovements good miles in rear POESTEERT.	
	7th		Leaving two certains at Brigade Headquarters T.27.a.26 and billets on Headquarters T.25.a.32 and T.19.b.93. Heavy aeroplane bombing attack on BAILLEUL completed	
	8th 10th		Clearing the form road NEUVE EGLISE. Salving and erecting camouflage at T.26.b.1.4.	

Army Form C. 2118.

WAR DIARY
or
INTELLIGENCE SUMMARY.
(Erase heading not required.)

Instructions regarding War Diaries and Intelligence Summaries are contained in F. S. Regs., Part II. and the Staff Manual respectively. Title pages will be prepared in manuscript.

Place	Date	Hour	Summary of Events and Information	Remarks and references to Appendices
	Sept			
	12th		Erecting cook house, latrine and English shelter at Brigade Headquarters T.22.c.4.6.	
	15th		2nd Lt. Busfield left on leave to PARIS.	
	16th		Salvage material and bonding at STEENWERCK dump and erecting English shelter at GOUGH HOUSE B.10.b.9.2., B.10.b.70.78., B.4.J.55.10. Erecting English shelter at Batt. Headquarters T.27.a.3.6. Erecting English shelter in the NIEPPE system. T.27.a.4.9. and preparing and resetting cook house standings at S.27.c.3.6.	
	17th Fri		2nd Lt. Parker returned from leave to U.K. Excavating for horse gun pits in NIEPPE system. T.27.c.8.1. Collecting material for horse standings at S.27.c.8.6.	
	19th		Constructing bridge to horse standings S.27.c.8.6. Capt. Clarke to XIIth Corps Rest, HARDELOT PLAGE.	
	21st			
CAESTRE	22nd		Company handed over 4 sector moved to CAESTRE. Handing over forward work to 2/6th Field Coy. and began work on arrival at CAESTRE. Repairing billets also 79, 108 and 24 (C.R.E) Repairing White Chateau also extern permanent at S.27.c.8.6 centenary on horse lines.	

Army Form C. 2118.

WAR DIARY
or
INTELLIGENCE SUMMARY.
(Erase heading not required.)

Instructions regarding War Diaries and Intelligence Summaries are contained in F. S. Regs., Part II. and the Staff Manual respectively. Title pages will be prepared in manuscript.

Place	Date	Hour	Summary of Events and Information	Remarks and references to Appendices
	Sept.			
	25th		Major Mansel M.C. R.E. left on leave to U.K.	
	26th		Refitting Coys 13, 14 and 15 Fields	
	27th		Lt Winfield returned from PARIS.	
	28th		Refitting Church and having rifles tested before an inspection on Monday.	
S.27.c.8.6	29th		Company moved forward to S.27.c.8.6. Relative map of GOUGH HOUSE	
	30th		Employing fields in camp and assisting in horse standings. at 4.45 p.m. Nos 2 and 4 sections with Lt Foster, proceeded by lorry, with further orders to proceed away S.30.b.3.4.	

J. E. Winfield
2nd Lt R.E.
211th Field Coy

WAR DIARY
OF THE
21ᵀᴴ FIELD COMPANY R.E.

FROM OCTOBER 1ˢᵗ TO OCTOBER 31ˢᵗ 1915

ORIGINAL

(VOLUME $\frac{III}{XXIV}$)

Army Form C. 2118.

WAR DIARY
or
INTELLIGENCE SUMMARY.
(Erase heading not required.)

Instructions regarding War Diaries and Intelligence Summaries are contained in F.S. Regs., Part II and the Staff Manual respectively. Title pages will be prepared in manuscript.

Place	Date	Hour	Summary of Events and Information	Remarks and references to Appendices
BAILLEUL	1.10.18		No. 2 Sect. making good PLOEGSTEERT – WARNETON road for heavy traffic.	
"	2.10.18		No. 1 Sect. screening NEUVE EGLISE Road from T.20.c.5.0. to T.15.a.0.5.	
"	3.10.18		As for the 1st. Transport lines moved to T.25.A.0.2. Nos. 2 and 4 Sects. move to forward camp at T.29.d.9.3. No. 2 Sect. making new wire PLOEGSTEERT Road at T.26.b.7.3.	
" (T.25.A.0.2)	4.10.18		Relieving weighing apparatus and screening. U.21.a.7.0. No. 2 Sect. completed diversion round wire at T.26.b.7.3. No. 4 Sect. made steps to Pill Box No. 15 at road – screen L.7 and downloading Pill Box.	
"	5.10.18		No. 2 Sect. Repairing light Railway running down to PLOEGSTEERT WOOD. Company 3 making the L.5 in S. Road, standing by to build the T.25.C.1.3.	
"	6.10.18		Building new camp at T.25.c.1.3.	
"	7.10.18		Co. for 5th Sept.	
"	8.10.18		Co. for 5th also wire making + placing with ditto	
"	9.10.18		Do. for 5th	

WAR DIARY
or
INTELLIGENCE SUMMARY

Army Form C. 2118.

(Erase heading not required.)

Oct 1918   2/1 K Field Coy RE

Place	Date	Hour	Summary of Events and Information	Remarks and references to Appendices
BAILLEUL T.25.a.0.2 10"18			Capt 5th No.4 Sect. went forward to L.13. to launch rafts, across a trench.	NK
"	11.10.18		Capt. No 5th in L.	
"	12.10.18		Capt. No. 6th in L.	
"	13.10.18		Capt. No 5th in L.	
"	14.10.18		Capt No 5th Capt W. INGRAM took over command from Capt T.N.K. LAWRIE	
"	15.10.18		During Latter's absence on leave. N/E	
"	16.10.18		Capt. No 5th No.3 Sect moved to T.29.d.9.3	
			Capt No 5th N/E taking up works re L.F.3 or rafts (1 night) N/E	
			Nos 2 and 4 Sects constructing a wilson piece bridge over the	
PLOEGSTEERT 17/10/18			MEUSE L.13 at POINT ROUGE. H.Q. and Transport moved to	
T.29.d.9.3			T.29.d.9.3 N/E	
QUESNOY 18.10.18			Coy moved to QUESNOY. Nos 2+4 Sects commencing work on bridge at QUESNOY. N/E	
			the Army traffic over the river. DEULE at QUESNOY.	
			Sects continued work on bridge over the DEULE	
WASQUEHAL 19.10.18			Transport and Nos 1+3 Sects march to WASQUEHAL arriving 2 p.m	
			Nos 2+4 Sects completed bridge at QUESNOY + then reported to Coy N/E	

Army Form C. 2118.

WAR DIARY
or
INTELLIGENCE SUMMARY.
(Erase heading not required.)

Oct. 1918   211th Field Coy R.E.

Place	Date	Hour	Summary of Events and Information	Remarks and references to Appendices
FRESTOY	21.10.18		Coy. marched to FRESTOY arriving about 1.30 p.m. the	
FRESTOY	22.10.18		Nos. 2 & 3 Sects returned to PONT ROUGE dismantled and salved timber &	
			Heldon trestles etc.	
"	23.10.18		Reconnaissance of HECHIN bridge	
"	24.10.18		Sections returned to FRESTOY. No. 2 taking bridging equipment &	
			repaired and landed sown to the 2/2 Aust. Tun. Coy R.E.	
COUERNE	25.10.18		Coy. marched to COUERNE arriving about 8 p.m. via Hulluch	
"	26.10.18		Gardening & leave. No work etc.	
HARLEBEKE	27.10.18		Coy marched to HARLEBEKE by motor bus	
"	28.10.18		No. 1 Sect moved to WINKEL St ELOI Reserves work by Lance Corps	
			Nos 2 & 3 gun material to tasks	
"	29.10.18		No. 1 on 28th & R.I.E.	
"	30.10.18		Nos. 2 on 28th Nos. 3. contd	
NICHTE	31.10.18		No. 1 Sect moved forward to NICHTE. No. 2 and 3 contd work at by-pass	
			forward to NICHTE. N.E.	

(Sd.) [signature] Maj
211th FIELD COMPANY R.E.

CONFIDENTIAL.

WAR DIARY

of

211th Field Company. R.E.

From 1/11/18 to 30/11/18.

VOLUME ~~III~~ XXXV

ORIGINAL.

WAR DIARY or INTELLIGENCE SUMMARY

Army Form C. 2118.

2nd/1st FIELD Coy R.E.

Oct. 1918

Place	Date	Hour	Summary of Events and Information	Remarks and references to Appendices
NIGHTE	1st		No.1 Sect. making blank forms transport cards etc - Pier Ent Section. No.3 Sect. collecting samples of water. Remainder of Coy. cleaning rifles etc. W/C	
"	2nd		As for 1st. Received wages for shoeing pers. for horses now here. W/C	
NIGHTE HALLUIN	3rd 4th		Coy moved off from NIGHTE 07.30.00 and arrived at HALLUIN about 17.00. W/C Cleaning + refitting rifles etc. W/C	
"	5th 6th		Sections practised in unpacking + assembling of Weldon Trestles. W/C As for 5th. W/C	
"	7th		Coy practised pontooning on Canal. W/C	
"	8th		No.3 Section marched to STEENBRUGGE to work at dump. Remaining sections drilling + practising with Weldon trestle. W/C	
SNEVEGHEM	9th		Coy marched to SNEVEGHEM arriving about 11 am. Nos 1, 2 + 4 Sects. billeted to RUGGE by lorry to work on plank road. HdQr + Transport marched to AVELGHEM. No.3 Sect. remained at STEENBRUGGE dump. W/C	

WAR DIARY
or
INTELLIGENCE SUMMARY.

(Erase heading not required.)

Army Form C. 2118.

Place	Date	Hour	Summary of Events and Information	Remarks and references to Appendices
HELGHEM	10th		Coy (Coy Hd.3 Sect) marched to AMOUGIES - arriving 3.30 pm. Coy Sect. refound road in AMOUGIES.	
REMUA	11th		Coy (less Nos 3 Sect) marched from AMOUGIES to 2 Sect sent forward to be nearer work. 1.15 a.m. Sects. Moving on reconnaissance in RENAIX-ELLEZELLES road. Commence cement of duties at 11.30. No 3 Sect. repaired Coy at 12.00 noon M.T.	
"	12th		Coy Karried at 10.30 am and was ordered in A.M. to No 3 house on ROUTE 31st Brig WC.	
"	13th		Nules on billots had removed every tile about that	
"	14th		Prepared returns to get ambuled bridge at MT in M.2	
"	15th		Cleaning and repairing material to complete plan of Bridge at X 17.b. and	
"	16th		Coy active in two shifts worked on ordso at XII.5 ptc.	
"	17th		Coy for 16th NIL	
"	18th		Coy for 16th NIL	
"	19th		Bridge at X 17.b. completed RE.C.	
RENAIX-KNONNE	20th		Marched from RENAIX and Athalie for reg.H. at KNONNE-KNOT	

WAR DIARY
or
INTELLIGENCE SUMMARY

(Erase heading not required.)

Army Form C. 2118

Instructions regarding War Diaries and Intelligence Summaries are contained in F. S. Regs., Part II. and the Staff Manual respectively. Title Pages will be prepared in manuscript.

May 18

Place	Date	Hour	Summary of Events and Information	Remarks and references to Appendices
MOORE – LAUWE	21st		Marched from MOORE to LAUWE.	
LAUWE	22nd		Coy on ceremonial drill.	
"	23rd		Coy attended lecture on "Demolitions"	
"	24th		Weapons and equipment cleaned and overhauled.	
LAUWE – MENIN	25th		Marched from LAUWE to MENIN.	
MENIN – YPRES	26th		Marched from MENIN to YPRES.	
YPRES – STEENVOORDE	27th		Marched from YPRES to STEENVOORDE.	
STEENVOORDE – STAPLE	28th		Marched from STEENVOORDE to STAPLE.	
STAPLE – ST OMER	29th		Marched from STAPLE to ST. OMER.	
ST OMER	30th		Rehearsing + improving billets.	

COMMANDING
211TH FIELD COMPANY R.E.

ORIGINAL.

CONFIDENTIAL.

WAR DIARY

of

211th Field Company. R.E.

From 1/12/18 to 31/12/18.

VOLUME ~~III~~ XXXIV

WAR DIARY or INTELLIGENCE SUMMARY

Army Form C. 2118

Dec. 1918

Place	Date	Hour	Summary of Events and Information	Remarks and references to Appendices
ST OMER	1st		Making furniture for Active Service Army Schools and for Company institutions. M.E.	
"	2nd		Do. for 1st M.C.	
"	3rd		Do. for 1st M.C.	
"	4th		Do. for 1st M.C.	
"	5th		Do. for 1st M.C.	
"	6th		Do. for 1st M.C.	
"	7th		Rehearsal for inspection of Division R.E. by G.O.C. sent Div. M.E. Church Parade. M.E.	
"	8th		Do. for 1st M.C.	
"	9th		As for 1st M.C. Rehearsal for G.O.C's inspection M.E.	
"	10th		The Coy. was bathed and all blankets & clothing were disinfected M.E.	
"	11th		Do. for 1st M.C.	
"	12th		Do. for 1st M.C.	
"	13th		Inspection of Div. of R.E. and presentation of medals by G.O.C. 57th Div. M.E.	
"	14th		Maj. R.F.S. Vance M.C., R.E. relinquished command of the Coy. M.E.	

Army Form C. 2118

WAR DIARY
or
INTELLIGENCE SUMMARY

(Erase heading not required.)

Dec. 1918   211th Field Coy R.E.

Instructions regarding War Diaries and Intelligence Summaries are contained in F.S. Regs., Part II. and the Staff Manual respectively. Title Pages will be prepared in manuscript.

Place	Date	Hour	Summary of Events and Information	Remarks and references to Appendices
SOMER	15th		Church Parade W.C.	
"	16th		No 1 Sect. pushing course for 31st Div. Mounted Sports. No 3 Sect erecting huts at 92nd Inft Bde camp. Remainder making furniture for U.S. Army Schs and barrack rooms etc.	
"	17th		Do For 16th W.C.	
"	18th		Do For 16th W.C.	
"	19th		Do For 16th W.C.	
"	20th		Do For 16th W.C.	
"	21st		Do For 16th W.C.	
"	22nd		Inspection of arms & equipment. Church Parade W.C.	
"	23rd		No 3 Section erecting huts on 92nd Inft Bde Camp. Remainder working in Coy workshops. Checking of Multiplication stores commenced. W.C.	
"	24th		Do For 23rd W.C.	
"	25th		Church Parade W.C.	
"	26th		Do For 23rd W.C.	
"	27th		Do For 23rd W.C.	
"	28th		Do For 23rd W.C.	

Army Form C. 2118

WAR DIARY
or
INTELLIGENCE SUMMARY

(Erase heading not required.)

211th Field Coy RE

Dec 1915

Instructions regarding War Diaries and Intelligence Summaries are contained in F.S. Regs., Part II. and the Staff Manual respectively. Title Pages will be prepared in manuscript.

Place	Date	Hour	Summary of Events and Information	Remarks and references to Appendices
ST. OMER	29th		Church Parade M.C.	
"	30th		Go for 2.3rd W.C	
"	31st		Go for 2.3rd W.C	

M Mark Coyle
O.C. 211th Field Coy RE
for O.C. 211th Field Coy RE

WAR DIARY.

of the

2.1.1th. FIELD COMPANY R.E.

for the month of JANUARY 1919.

VOLUME XXXVII

Army Form C. 2118.

WAR DIARY
or
INTELLIGENCE SUMMARY.

(Erase heading not required.)

211 Field Company R.E.

Place	Date	Hour	Summary of Events and Information	Remarks and references to Appendices
	1919 JAN.			
ST OMER	1		Effective strength 7 Offrs 195 O.R.	
"	10		Maj. J. MASON M.C. R.E. assumed command	The unit throughout the month has undergone gradual demobilisation and has been engaged on erection and maintenance of camps and billets for Hdr. 38, 13 Div. & ST OMER
"	22		2nd Lieut. F. L. PARKIN demobilised	
"	26		Lieut. F. R. BURFIELD demobilised	
"	31		Effective strength 5 offrs (2 on course) 135 O.R.	

J Mason Maj R.E.
O.C. 211 F. Coy R.E.

WAR DIARY.

211th FIELD COMPANY, ROYAL ENGINEERS.

FEBRUARY, 1919.

Army Form C. 2118.

WAR DIARY
or
INTELLIGENCE SUMMARY.

(Erase heading not required.)

211th FIELD COY, R.E.

FEB. 1919

Place	Date	Hour	Summary of Events and Information	Remarks and references to Appendices
St. OMER	1st to 28th		Coy. billeted at St. OMER. Carrying out various repairs of Divisional Camps. Maj. J. MASON M.C, R.E. handed over command of Coy. to CAPT. J.W. CLARKE, R.E. on 23.2.19	

J.W. Clarke Capt. R.E.
O.C. 211th Field Coy. R.E.

Army Form C. 2118.

WAR DIARY
or
INTELLIGENCE SUMMARY.
(Erase heading not required.)

Instructions regarding War Diaries and Intelligence Summaries are contained in F. S. Regs., Part II. and the Staff Manual respectively. Title pages will be prepared in manuscript.

MARCH 1919   211th FIELD Co R.E.   Vol. 37

Place	Date	Hour	Summary of Events and Information	Remarks and references to Appendices
ST OMER	1st to 23rd		Carrying out R.E. work for 31st Division and St Omer District	
	to 31st		Checking, cleaning and packing Coy equipment and moving to transport to rail-head.	

Clarke Capt.
211th Field Coy R.E.

WAR DIARY
or
INTELLIGENCE SUMMARY

(Erase heading not required.)

Army Form C. 2118

April - 1919   211th Field Coy R.E.   30 38

Place	Date	Hour	Summary of Events and Information	Remarks and references to Appendices
St Omer	1st to 30th		The cadre of the Coy. waiting to proceed to H.Q. for dispersal. Equipment handed and weapons finished and tested at workshops under a guard. Carrying out small repairs etc. to road in the neighbourhood.	

[signed] Major
O.C. 211th Field Coy. R.E.

www.ingramcontent.com/pod-product-compliance
Lightning Source LLC
Chambersburg PA
CBHW081412160426
43193CB00013B/2159